PIANO / VOCAL / GUITAR

TOP COUNTRY HITS
2019-2020

T0055711

ISBN 978-1-5400-8511-5

HAL•LEONARD®

Visit Hal Leonard Online at
www.halleonard.com

Contact us:
Hal Leonard
7777 West Bluemound Road
Milwaukee, WI 53213
Email: info@halleonard.com

In Europe, contact:
Hal Leonard Europe Limited
42 Wigmore Street
Marylebone, London, W1U 2RN
Email: info@halleonardeurope.com

In Australia, contact:
Hal Leonard Australia Pty. Ltd.
4 Lentara Court
Cheltonham, Victoria, 3192 Australia
Email: info@halleonard.com.au

ALL TO MYSELF

Words and Music by DAN SMYERS,
JORDAN REYNOLDS, SHAY MOONEY
and NICOLLE GALYON

I'm jeal-ous of the blue jeans that you're wear - in',

and the way they're hold - in' you __ so tight. __

I'm jeal - ous of the moon that keeps on star - in',

Recorded a half step higher.

so lock the door ___ and turn out the night. ___ I want you

all to my-self. ___ We don't need an-y-one ___ else. ___ Let our bod-

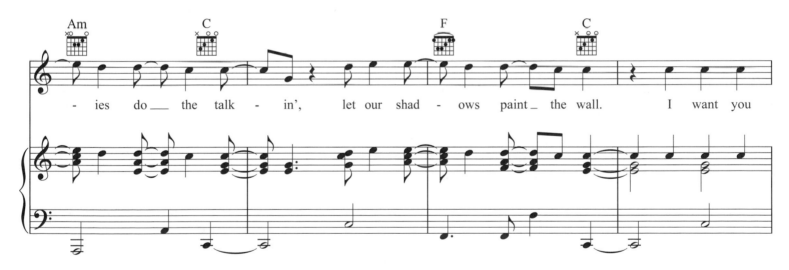

-ies do ___ the talk-in', let our shad-ows paint ___ the wall. I want you

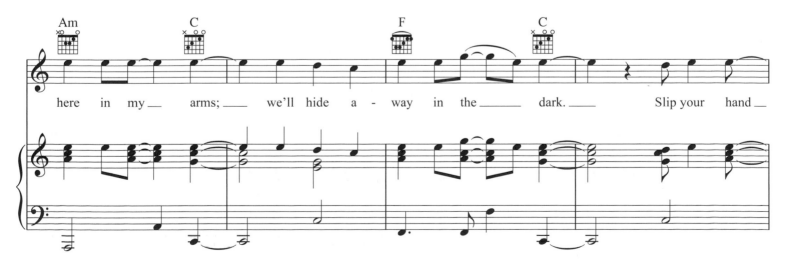

here in my ___ arms; ___ we'll hide a-way in the _____ dark. ___ Slip your hand ___

To Coda

in my back pock - et, go and let your long hair fall. I want you

all to my - self, to my - self.

I'm jeal-ous of the song that you've been sing - in'

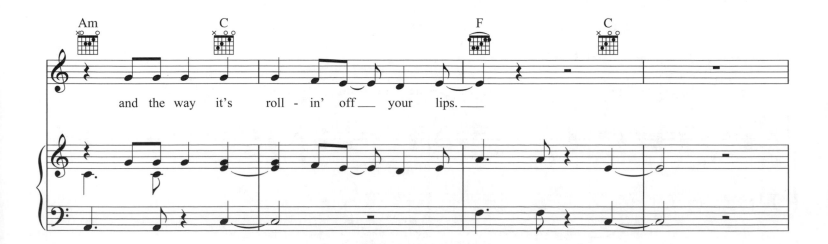

and the way it's roll - in' off your lips.

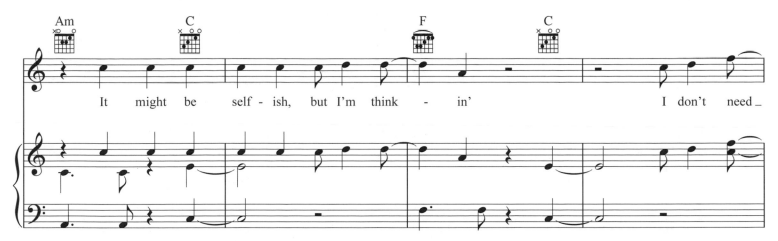

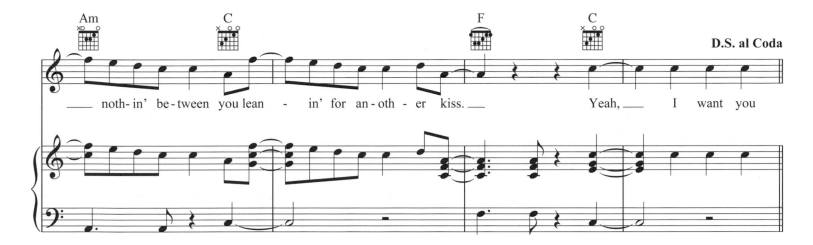

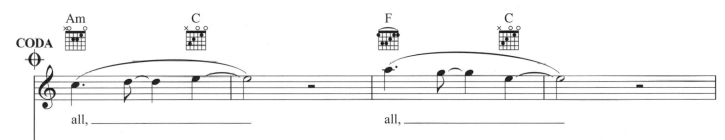

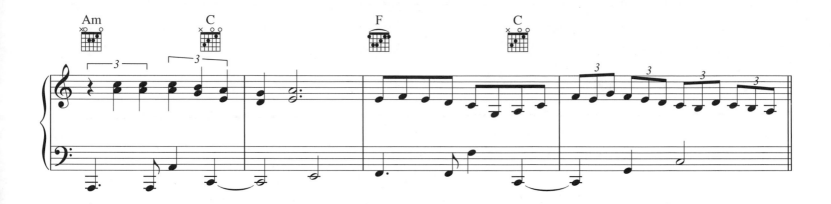

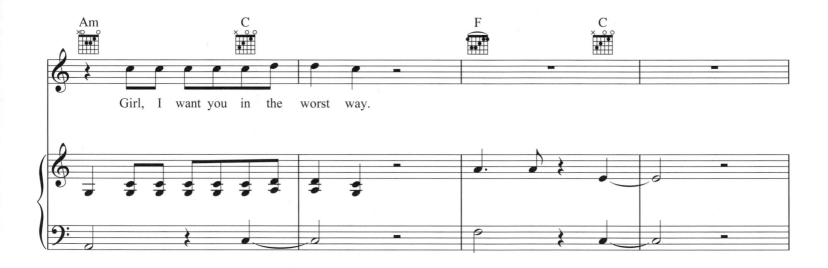

Girl, I want you in the worst way.

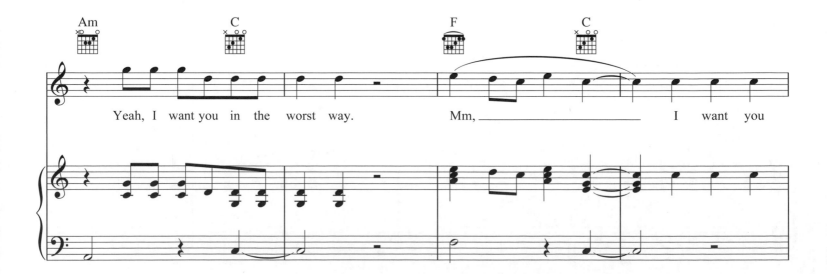

Yeah, I want you in the worst way. Mm, _____ I want you

all to my - self,____ we don't need an - y - one ____ else.____ Let our bod-

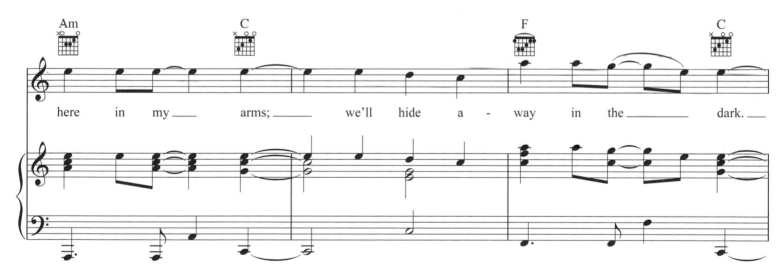

- ies do ____ the talk - in', let our shad - ows paint ___ the wall. I want you

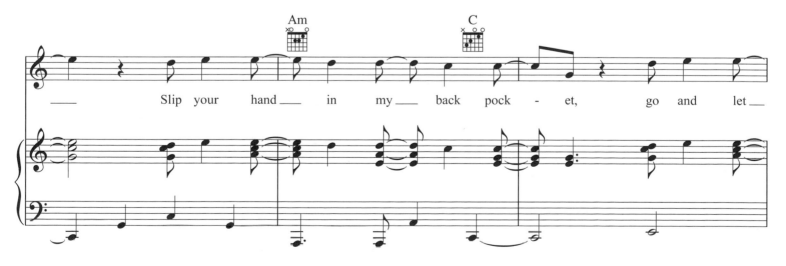

here in my ____ arms;____ we'll hide a - way in the _____ dark. ____

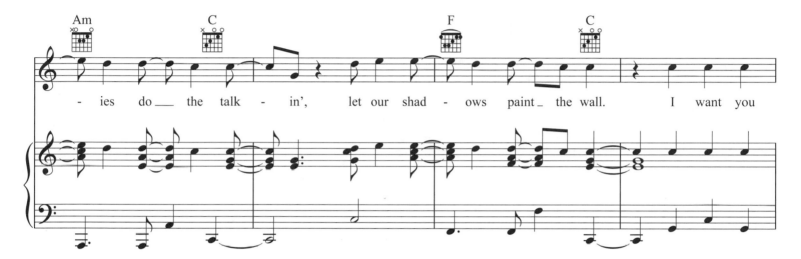

____ Slip your hand ____ in my ____ back pock - et, go and let ____

___ your long ___ hair fall. ___ I want you all, ___

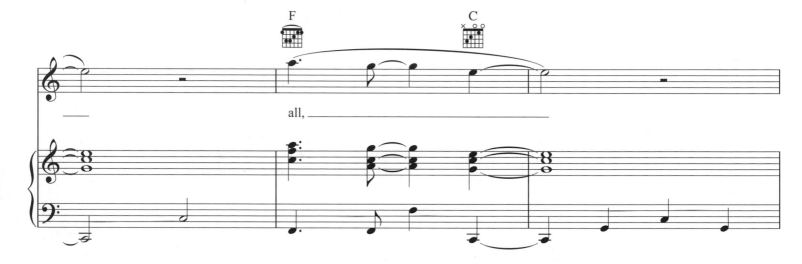

all, _____

all _____ to my - self, _____ to my - self. ___

___ I want you ___ to my - self, _____ yeah.

EVEN THOUGH I'M LEAVING

Words and Music by LUKE COMBS,
RAY FULCHER and WYATT DURRETTE

Moderately slow, in 2

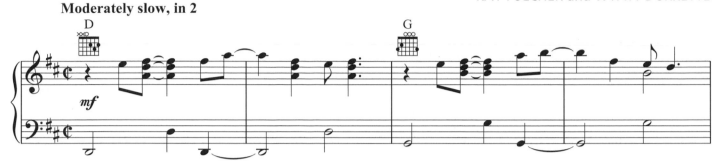

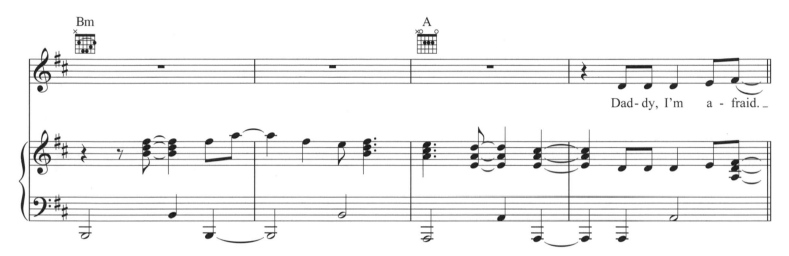

Dad-dy, I'm a-fraid.

Won't you stay _____ a lit-tle while? _____
and Un-cle Sam _____ don't like to wait. _____

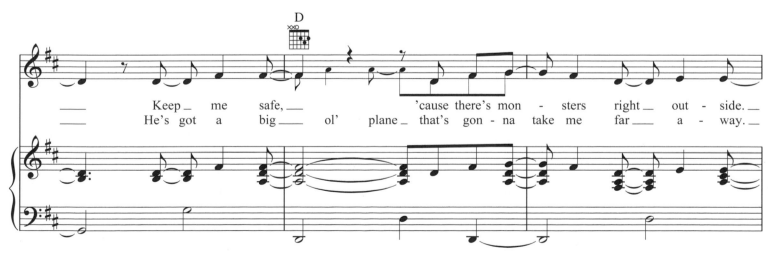

Keep _____ me safe, _____ 'cause there's mon-sters right _____ out-side. _____
He's got a big _____ ol' plane _____ that's gon-na take me far _____ a-way. _____

12

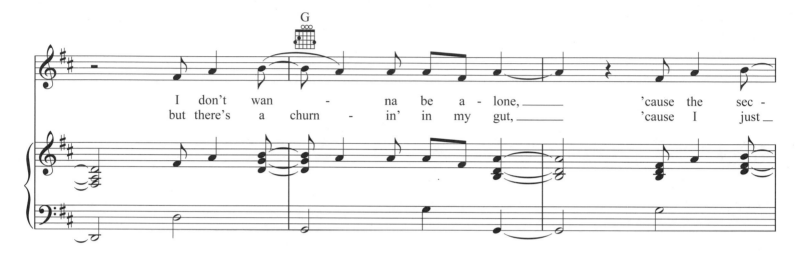

said, — "Just 'cause I'm } leav - in', it don't mean —
said, — "Just 'cause you're }

that I won't be — right by — your side — when you need —

me and you can't see — me in the mid - dle of — the — night. —

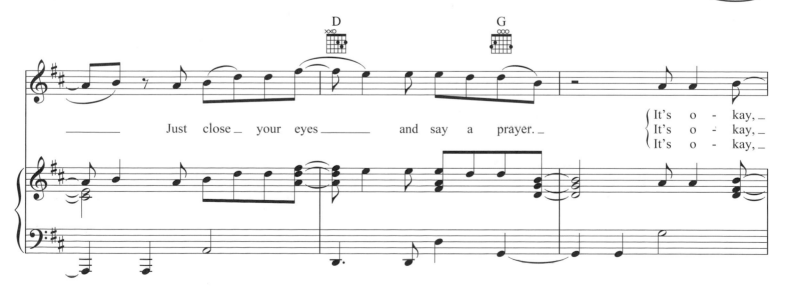

Just close — your eyes — and say a prayer. — It's o - kay, —
It's o - kay, —
It's o - kay, —

I know you're scared when I'm not here. But I'll al-
I know you're scared. I might be here, but I'll al-
boy, I ain't scared. I won't be here, but I'll al-

To Coda ⊕

-ways be right there.
-ways be right there.
-ways be right there.

E - ven though I'm } leav-
E - ven though you're }

-in', I ain't go - in' no - where."

Dad, we'll be late,

Dad - dy, I'm a - fraid. _

_____ Won't you stay _____ a lit - tle while? _

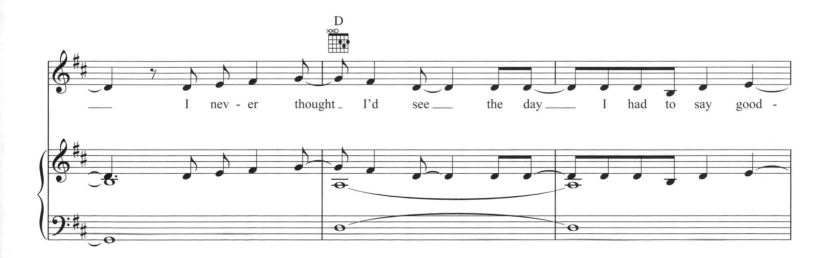

_____ I nev - er thought _ I'd see _ the day _ I had to say good -

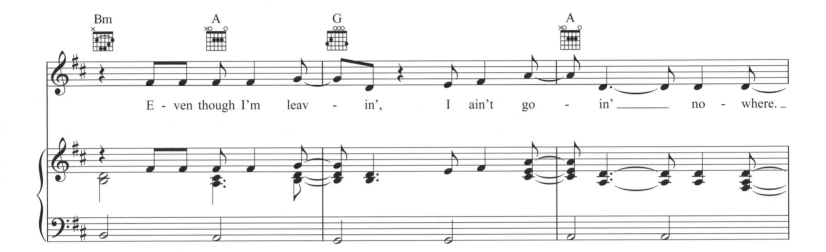

BEER NEVER BROKE MY HEART

Words and Music by LUKE COMBS,
JONATHAN SINGLETON and RANDY MONTANA

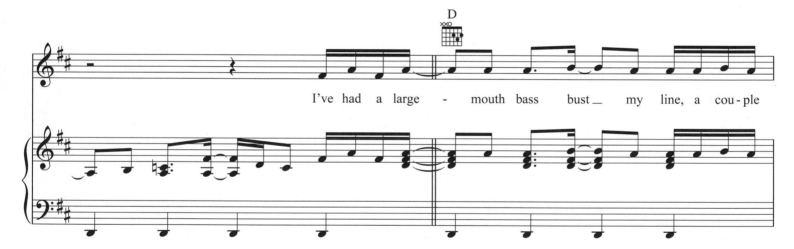

I've had a large - mouth bass bust __ my line, a cou - ple

beau - ti - ful girls __ tell me good - bye. Trucks __ break down, dogs __ run off, pol -

Recorded a half step lower.

- i -ti -cians lie, been fired by the boss. It takes one ___ hand to count the things I can

count ___ on. No, there ain't much, man, ___ that ain't nev -er let

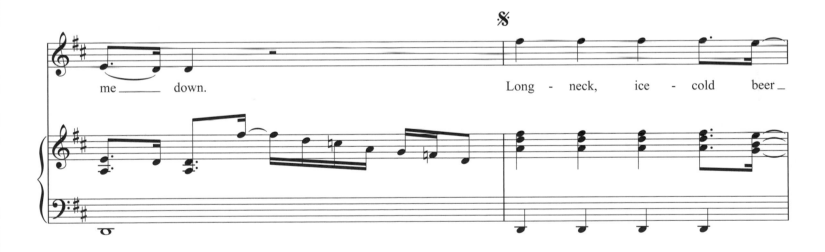

me ___ down. Long - neck, ice - cold beer ___

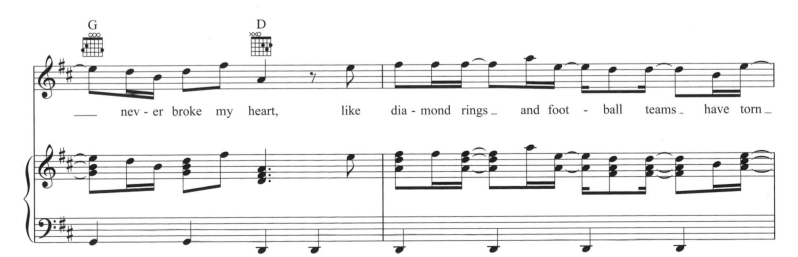

G   D

___ nev - er broke my heart, like dia -mond rings ___ and foot - ball teams ___ have torn ___

this boy a-part. __ Like a ne-on dream, __ it just dawned on me that

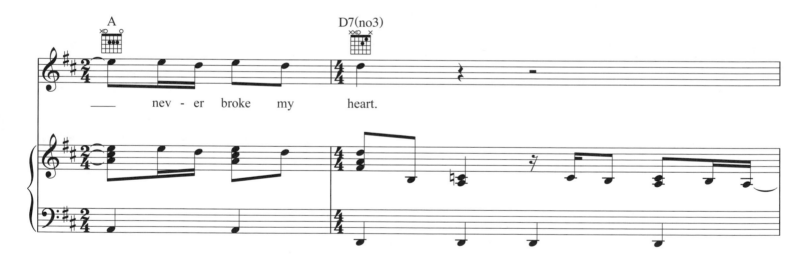

bars and this gui-tar __ and long-neck, ice-cold beer __

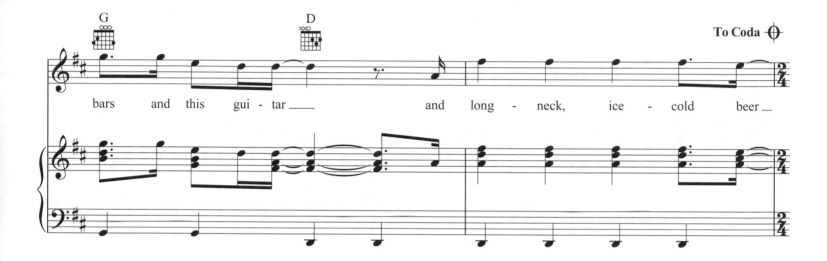

__ nev-er broke my heart.

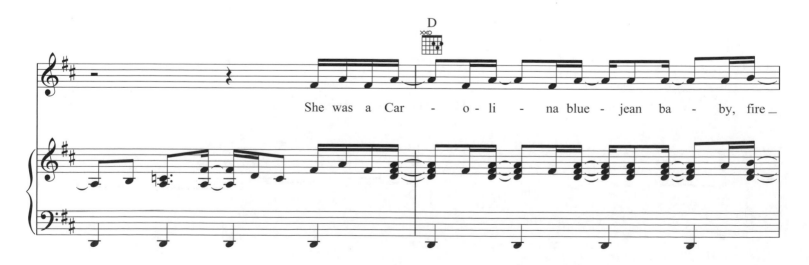

She was a Car-o-li-na blue-jean ba-by, fire __

in her eyes that drove me cra - zy. It was red tail-lights when she __ left town.__ If I

D.S. al Coda

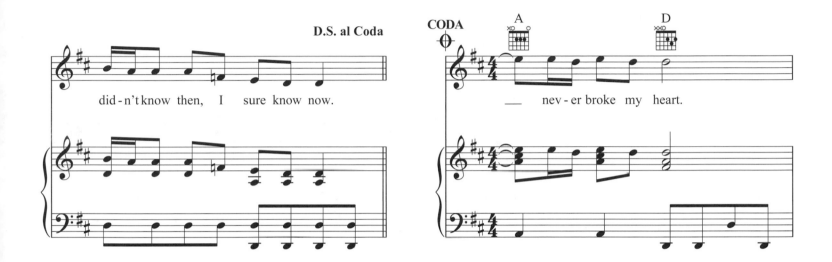

did-n't know then, I sure know now.

CODA

A   D

__ nev - er broke my heart.

G   D7(no3)   E

A   D

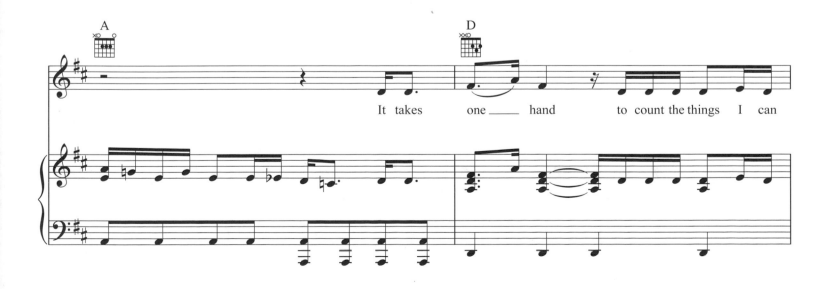

It takes   one __ hand   to count the things I can

count ___ on, but I got one hand ___ that's grip-pin' down on a

cold one. 'Cause long - neck, ice - cold beer ___

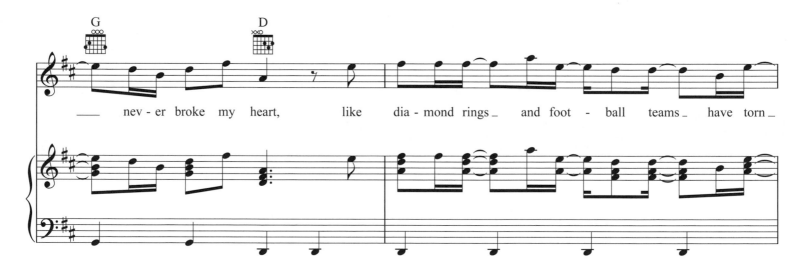

G   D

___ nev - er broke my heart, like dia-mond rings ___ and foot - ball teams ___ have torn ___

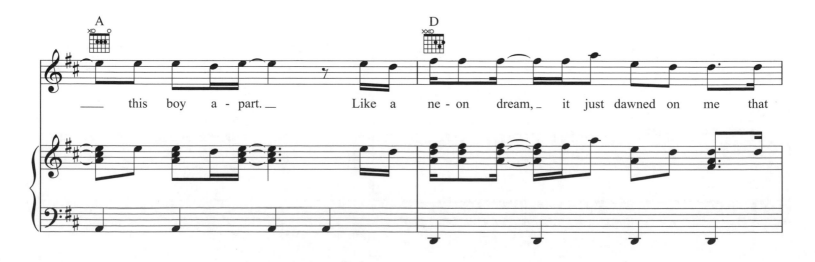

A   D

___ this boy a - part. ___ Like a ne - on dream, ___ it just dawned on me that

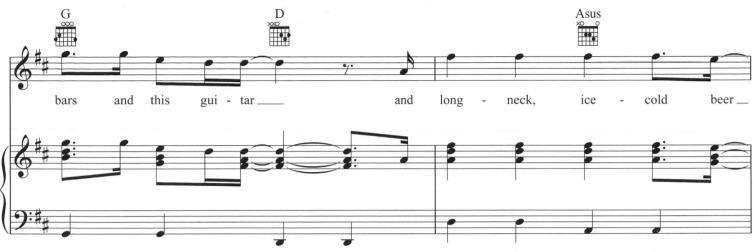

bars and this gui - tar _____ and long - neck, ice - cold beer _____

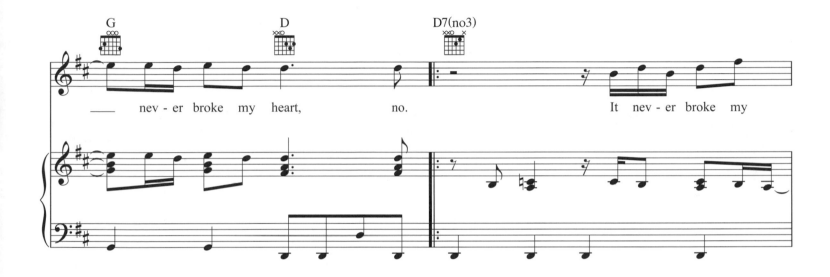

_____ nev - er broke my heart, no. It nev - er broke my

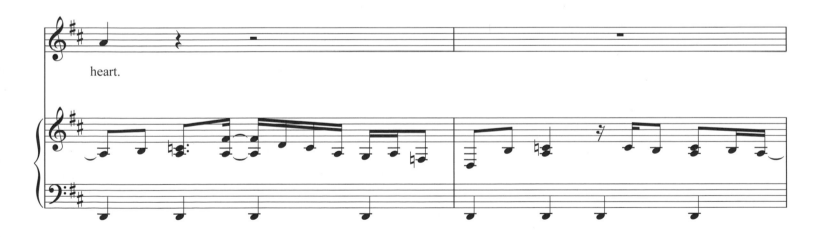

heart.

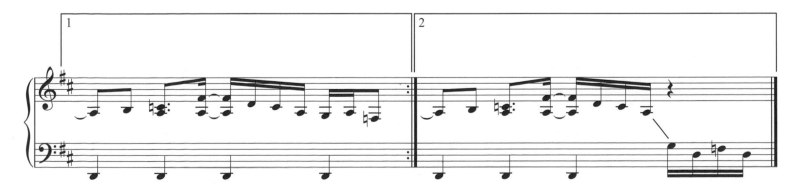

THE BONES

Words and Music by MAREN MORRIS,
JIMMY ROBBINS and LAURA VELTZ

Moderately slow, in 2

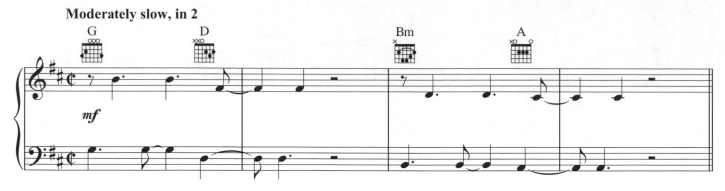

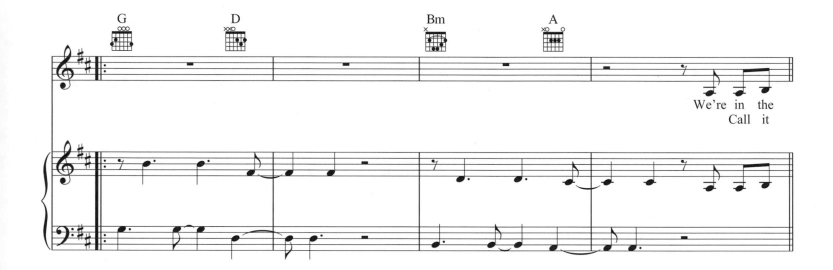

We're in the
Call it

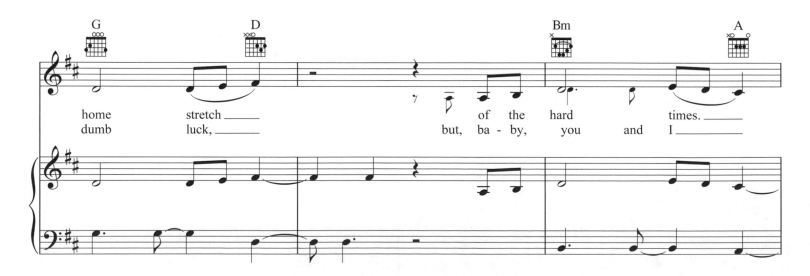

home   stretch _____   of the hard   times. _____
dumb   luck, _____   but, ba - by, you   and I _____

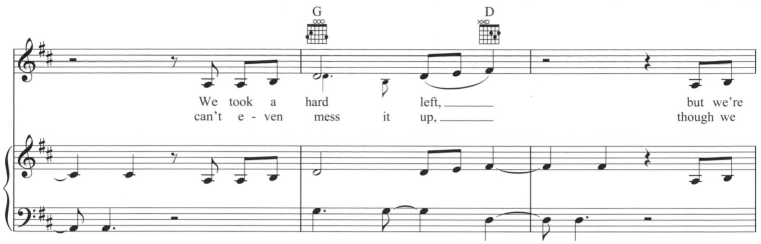

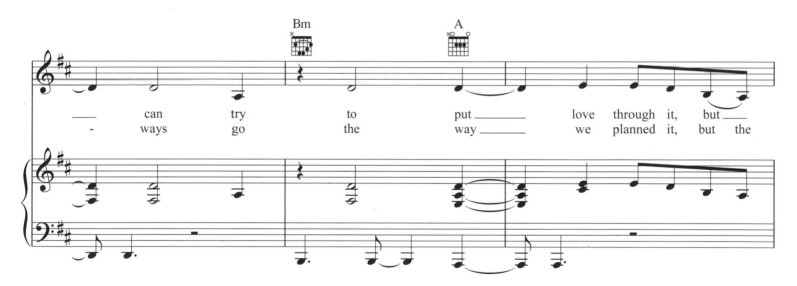

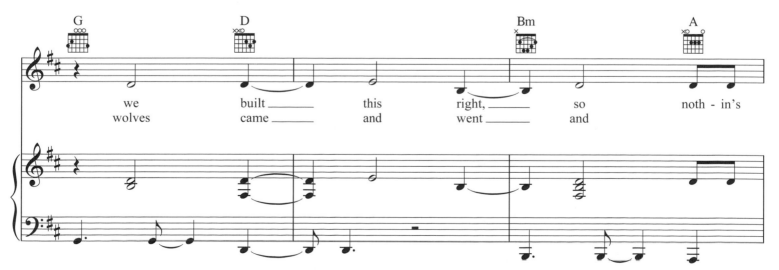

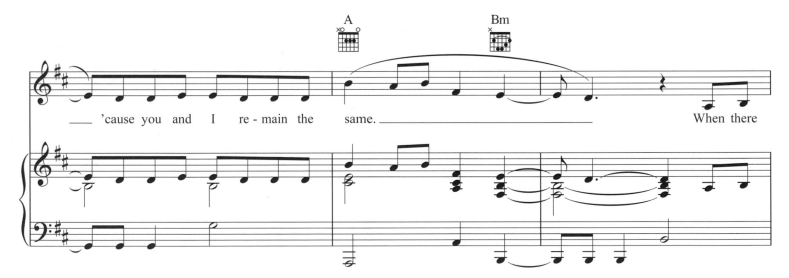

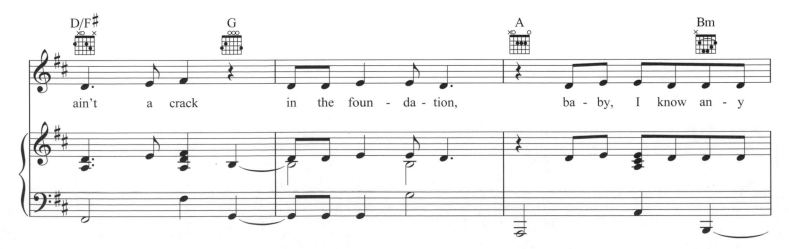

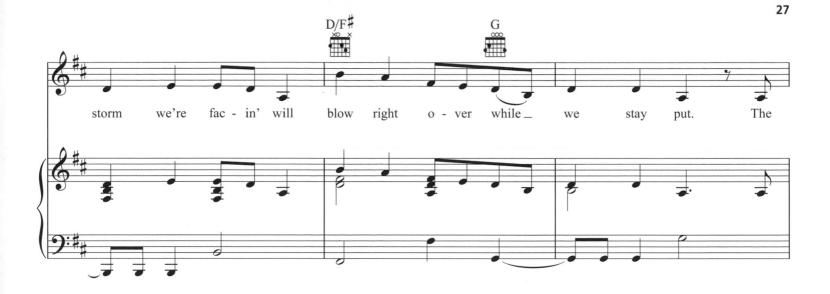

storm we're fac-in' will blow right o-ver while __ we stay put. The

house don't fall when the bones are good. bones are good.

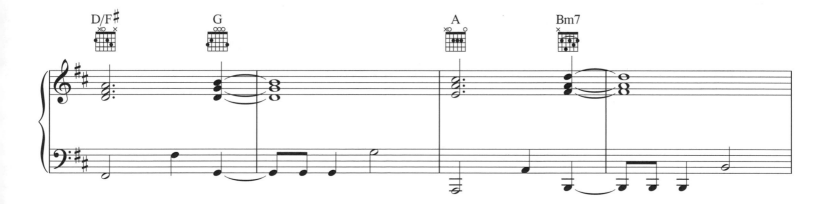

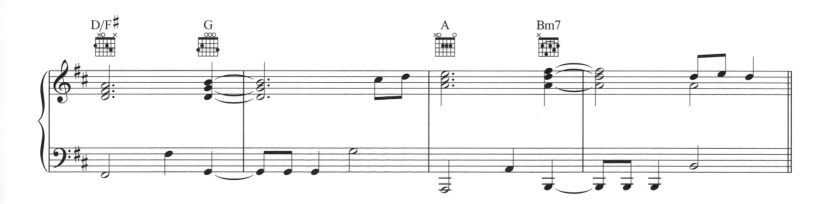

Bones are good, _____ the rest, _____ the

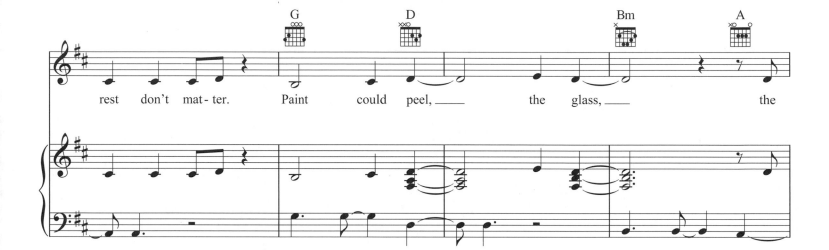

rest don't mat-ter. Paint could peel, _____ the glass, _____ the

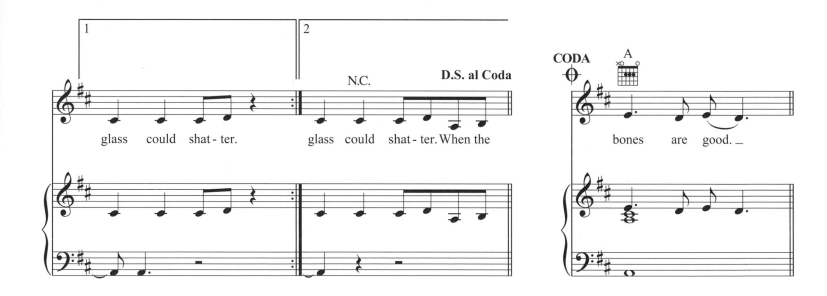

glass could shat-ter.

glass could shat-ter. When the

CODA

bones are good. _

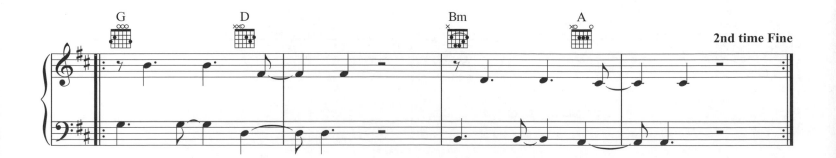

2nd time Fine

LOOK WHAT GOD GAVE HER

Words and Music by THOMAS RHETT,
AMMAR MALIK, JACOB HINDLIN,
JULIAN BUNETTA, JOHN RYAN
and RHETT AKINS

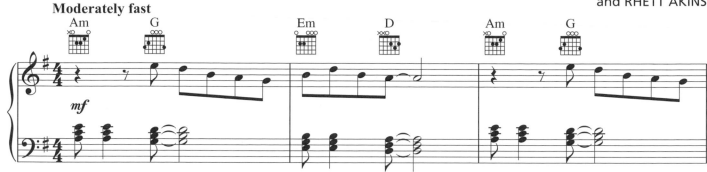

Don't e-ven want the at-ten-tion, but yeah, that's all that she's get-
It's like I heard an-gels sing-in', like she came down from the ceil-

tin'. Her song is on and she's spin-nin' a-round. __
in'. When she walked in here this eve-nin', I thought: _

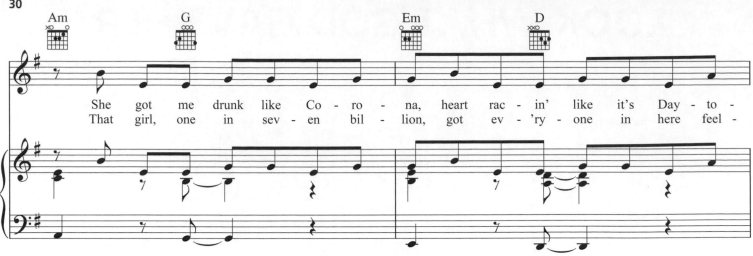

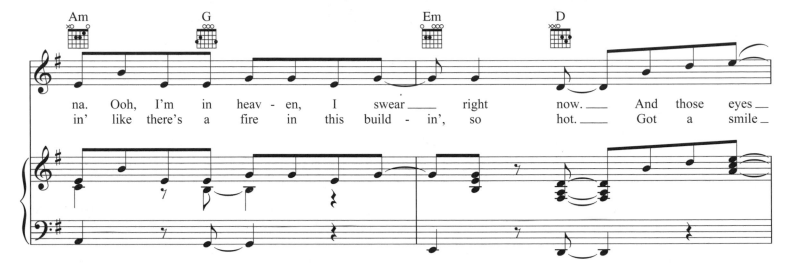

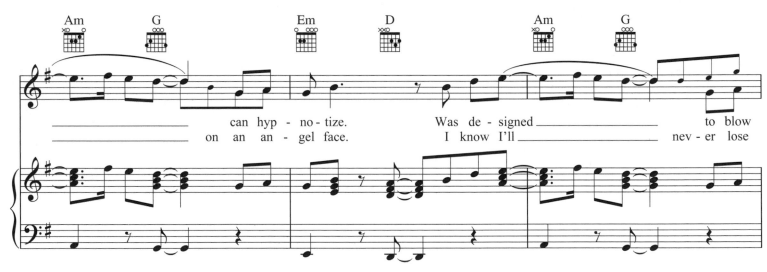

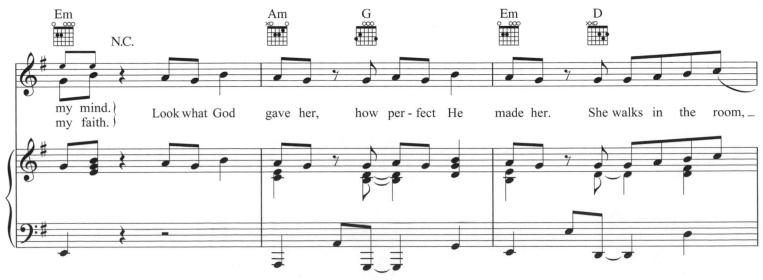

it's like He an-swered my prayers. ____ The way that she moves, ____ how could an-y-bod-y

blame her? I know she's got hat-ers, but it ain't her fault, nah. Look what God

gave her.

Got that look in her eye,

blame her? I know she's got hat - ers, but it ain't her fault, _____ nah.   Look what God

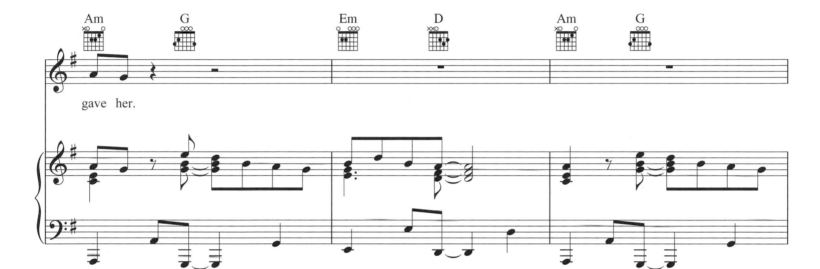

gave her.

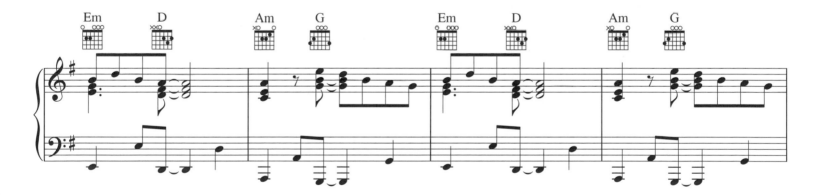

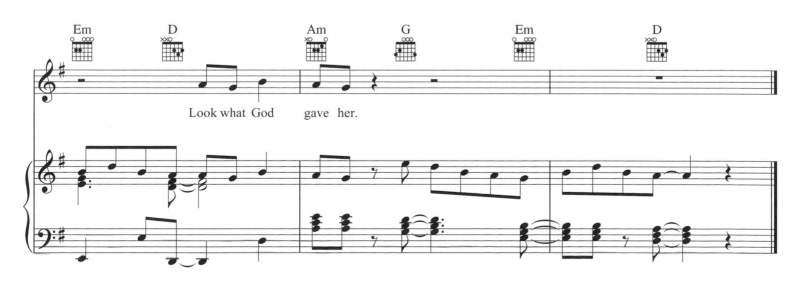

Look what God   gave her.

GIRL

Words and Music by MAREN MORRIS,
SARAH AARONS and GREG KURSTIN

Moderately slow

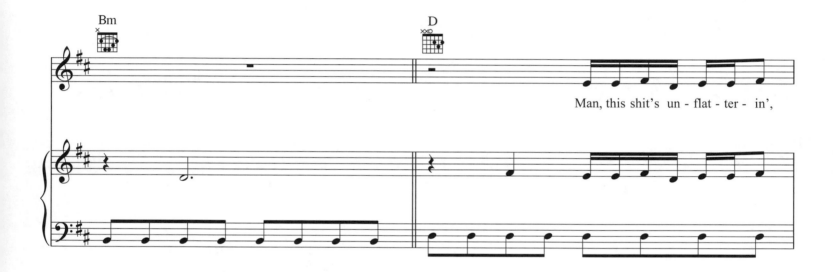

Man, this shit's un-flat-ter-in',

all up in my head a-gain.   I don't feel my-self right

* Recorded a half step lower.

ha - lo. Ev-'ry-one's gon-na be o - kay,__ ba - by__ girl.

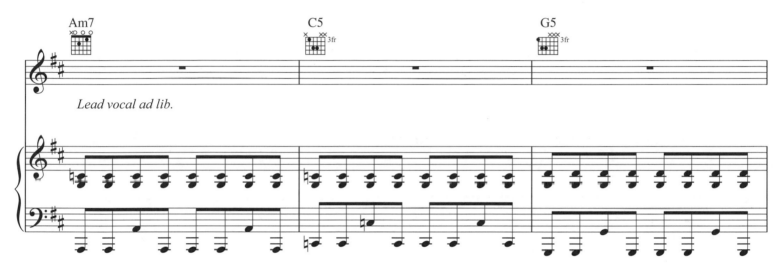

Lead vocal ad lib.

Girl, don't hang your head __ low. Don't lose your ha - lo, don't lose your ha - lo. _____

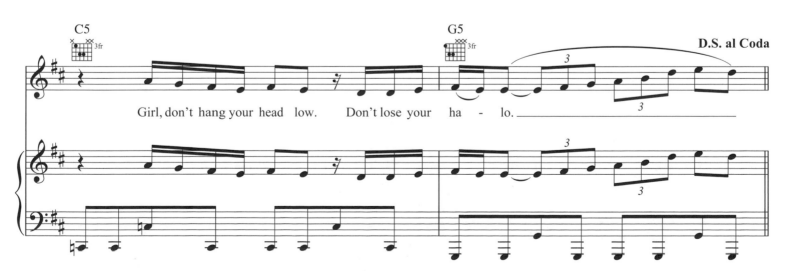

Girl, don't hang your head low. Don't lose your ha - lo. _____

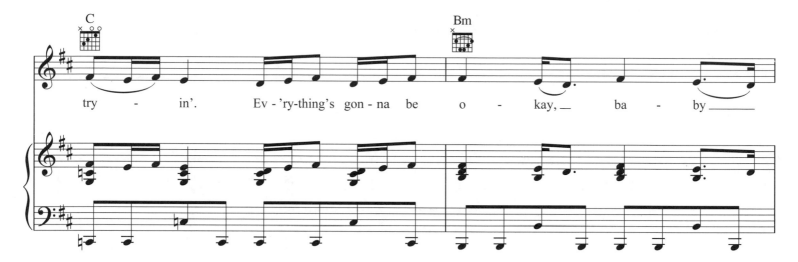

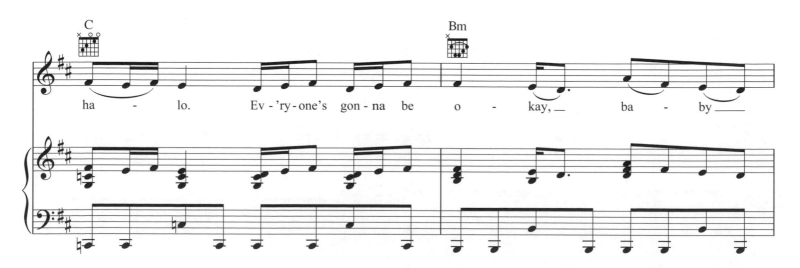

girl. Ev-'ry - one's gon-na be _____ o - kay, _____

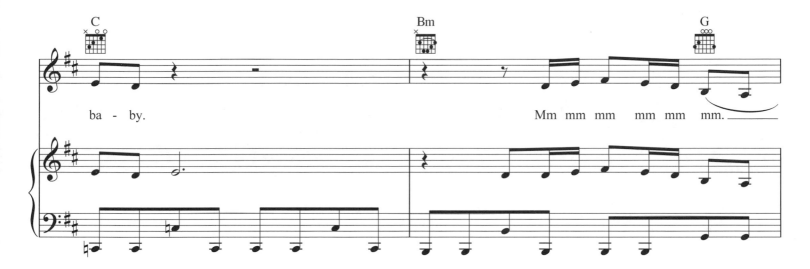

ba - by. Mm mm mm mm mm mm. _____

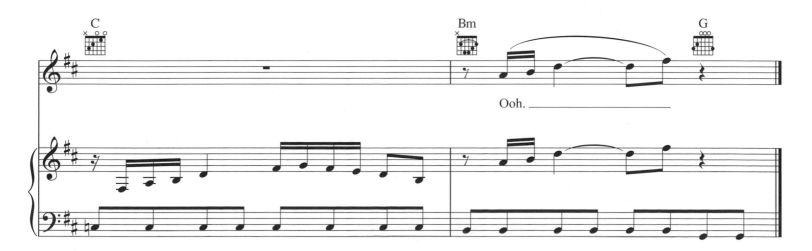

Ooh. _____

GOD'S COUNTRY

Words and Music by MICHAEL HARDY,
JORDAN SCHMIDT and DEVIN DAWSON

Moderately slow, in 2

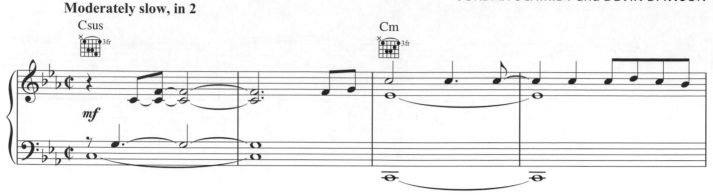

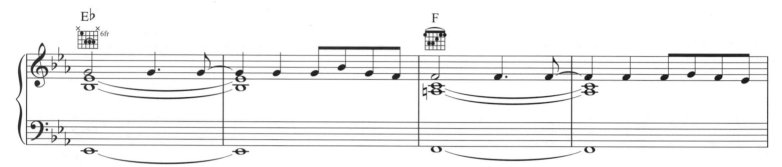

Right out-side __ of this one-church town there's a

gold dirt road to a whole lot-ta noth-in'. Got a deed to the land, but it

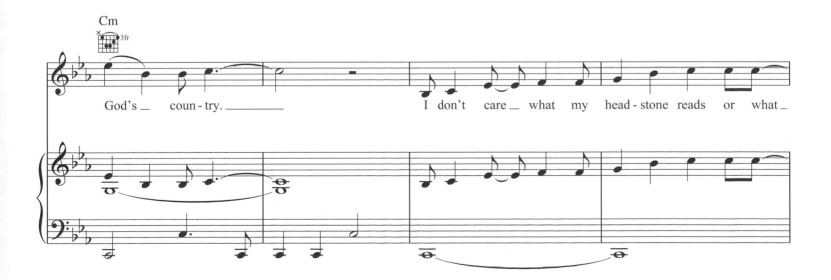

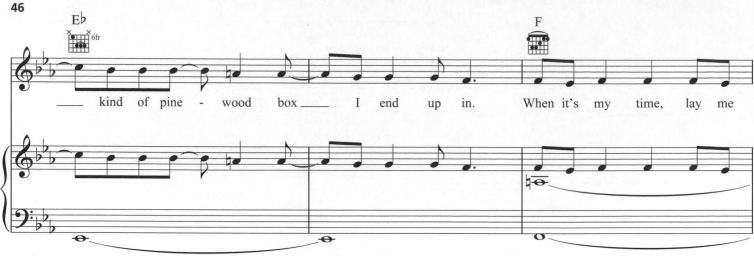

kind of pine - wood box ___ I end up in. When it's my time, lay me

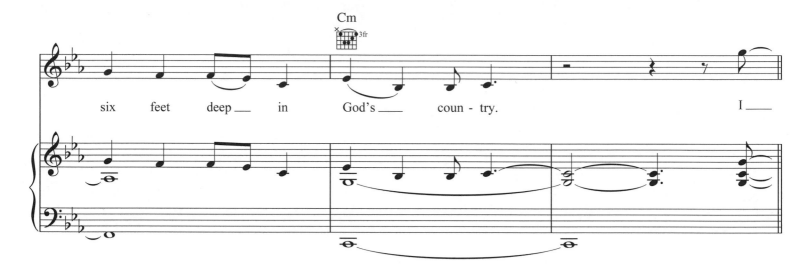

six feet deep ___ in God's ___ coun - try. I ___

saw the light ___ in a sun - rise sit - tin' back in a for - ty on the

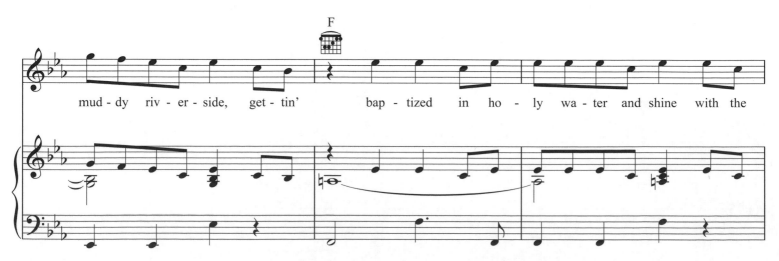

mud - dy riv - er - side, get - tin' bap - tized in ho - ly wa - ter and shine with the

I DON'T KNOW ABOUT YOU

Words and Music by MICHAEL HARDY,
JAMESON RODGERS, ASHLEY GORLEY
and HUNTER PHELPS

Moderately, in 2

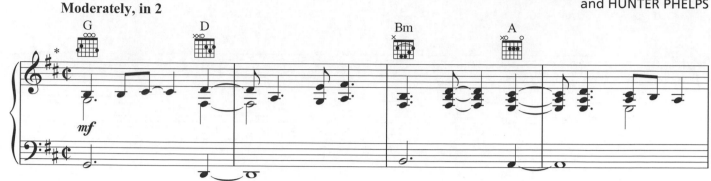

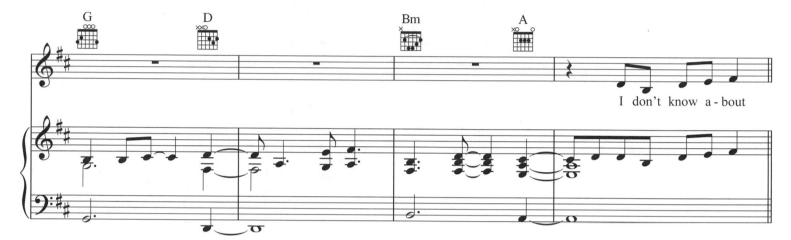

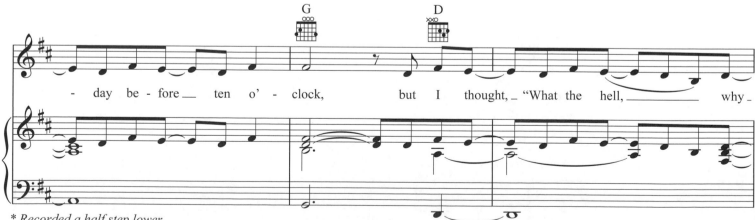

Recorded a half step lower.

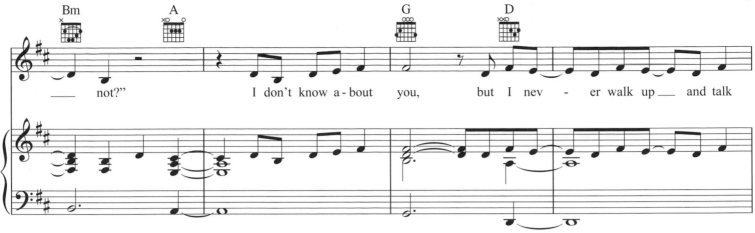

not?" I don't know a-bout you, but I nev - er walk up___ and talk

to a stran - ger, but when___ I saw___ you, I had___

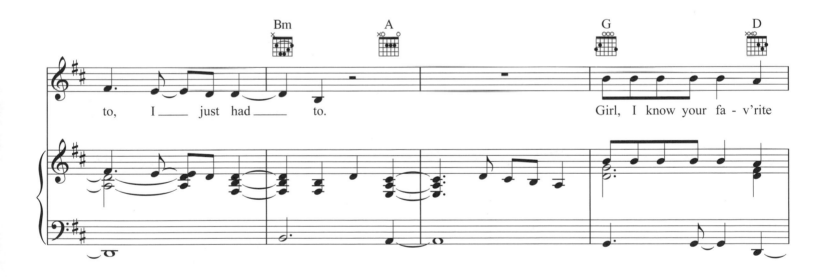

to, I___ just had___ to. Girl, I know your fa - v'rite

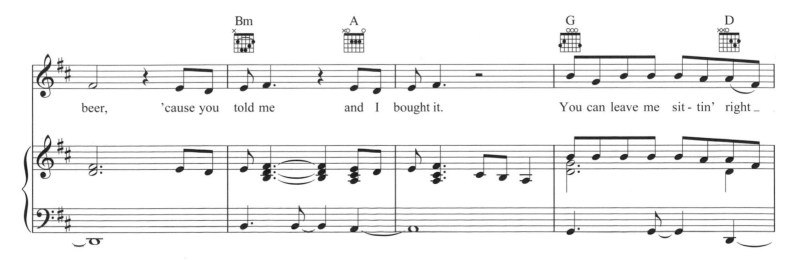

beer, 'cause you told me and I bought it. You can leave me sit - tin' right___

Yeah, what makes your world spin a - round and a - round?_ And are you down to get

out - ta here, too? Tell me ev - 'ry - thing till there's noth - in' I don't know a - bout

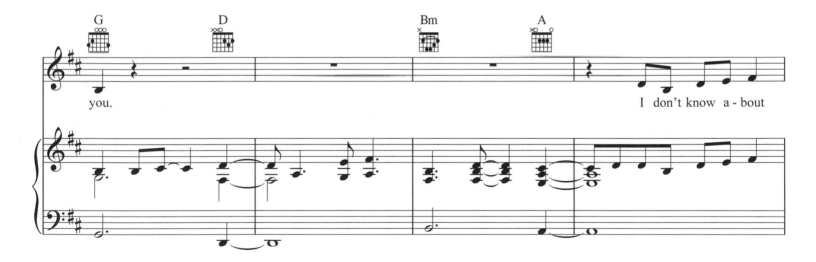

you. I don't know a - bout

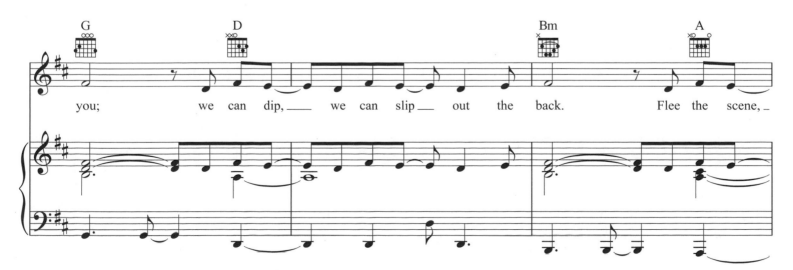

you; we can dip,_ we can slip_ out the back. Flee the scene,_

put your feet___ on my dash. Find a spot___ past the rail - road

tracks and nev - er look back.___ But be - fore_____ that, What's your name, what's your

sign, what's your birth - day?_____ What's your wrist tat - too Bi - ble verse say?

Tell me this: do you kiss on the first date? Don't hold an - y - thing

I know you like Bud ___ Light, I know you got blue ___ eyes, I know you got my

heart beat-in' in this bar. ___ To-night we can jump ___ in, fall in-to some-

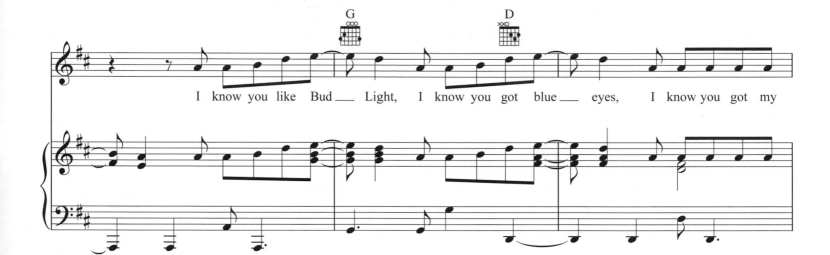

D.S. al Coda

- thin', and the per-fect place ___ to start ___ is...

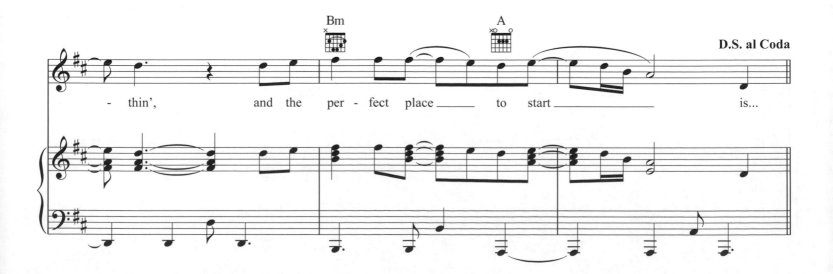

MISS ME MORE

Words and Music by KELSEA BALLERINI,
DAVID HODGES and BRETT McLAUGHLIN

ti-red my red lip-stick 'cause you said you did-n't like it. I did-n't

put on my old rec-ords that I hid in the back of the clos-et, and I

wear my high-heel shoes ' cause I could-n't be tall-er than you. I did-n't
turned them up to ten, and then I played them all a - gain. I

wan - na lose my friends, but now it's hard to e - ven find them. It's what you
found my in - de - pen - dence; can't be - lieve I ev - er lost it. It's what you

want - ed, ain't it? It's what you want - ed.
want - ed, ain't it? It's what you want - ed.

I thought I'd

Dm

Am

miss you __ (when it end - ed.) I thought it'd hurt me, __ (but it did - n't.) I thought I'd

miss you, ___ I thought I'd miss you, ___ but I miss me more.

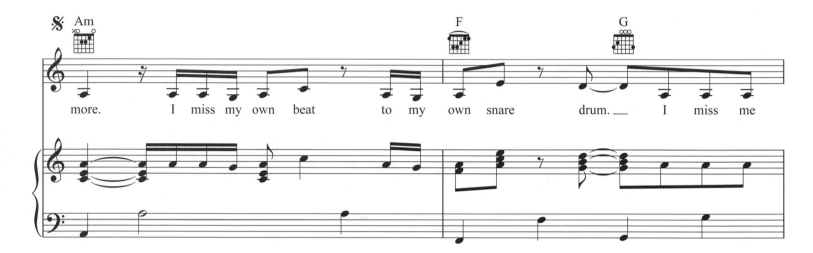

I miss my own beat to my own snare drum. ___ I miss me

more. I miss my own sheets in the bed I made up. ___ I for-

got I had dreams, I for-got I had wings, for-got who I was be-fore ___ I ev-er

kissed you. ___ Yeah, I thought I'd miss you, ___ but I miss me

more. (Ah, ___ ah, ___ ah.) ___ I miss me

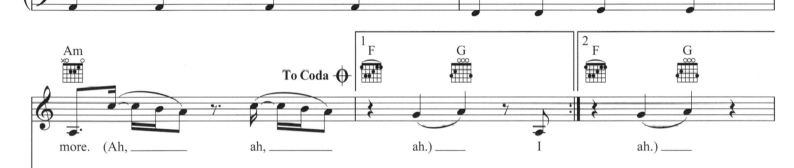

more. (Ah, ___ ah, ___ ah.) ___ I ah.) ___

I thought I'd

60

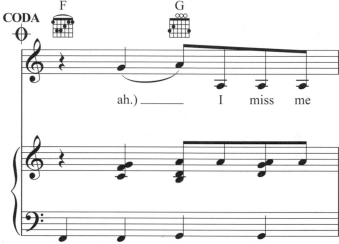

ONE MAN BAND

Words and Music by MATTHEW RAMSEY,
JOSH OSBORNE, BRAD TURSI
and TREVOR ROSEN

Moderately slow, in 2

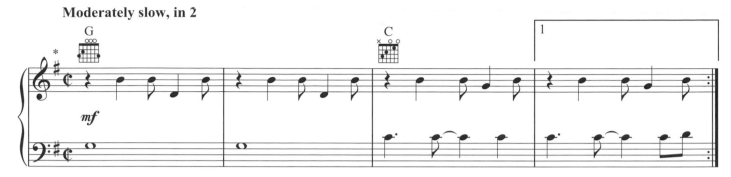

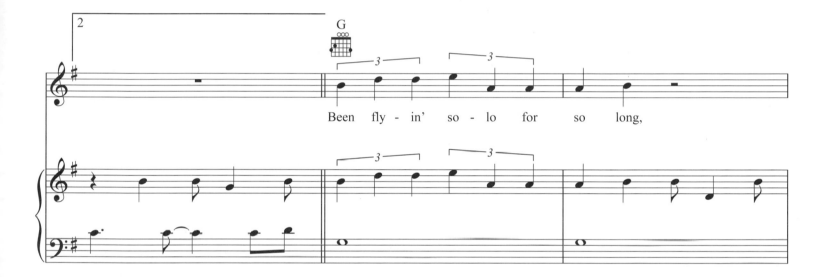

Been fly-in' so-lo for so long,

no-bod-y sing-in' the har-mo-ny.   Up there, just me and my

Recorded a half step lower.

shad - ow. No bass, no gui - tar, no tam - bou - rine.

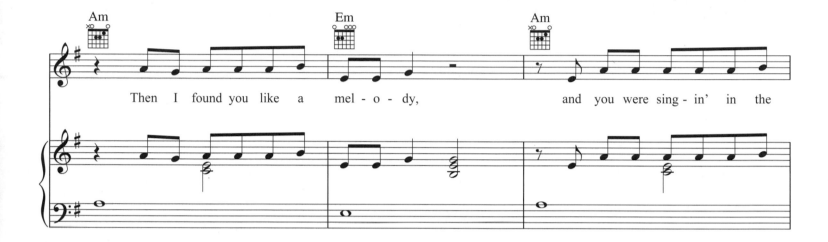

Then I found you like a mel - o - dy, and you were sing - in' in the

same key as me. We had 'em danc - in' in the streets. I don't wan - na be a

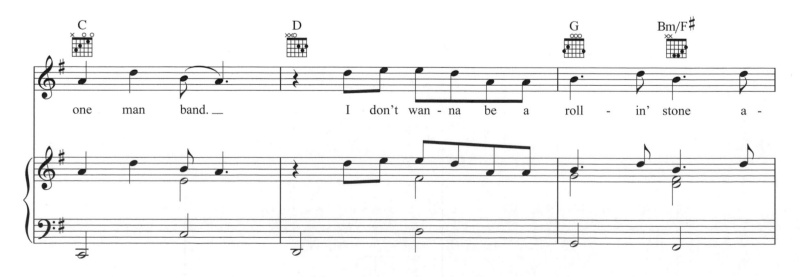

one man band. __ I don't wan - na be a roll - in' stone a -

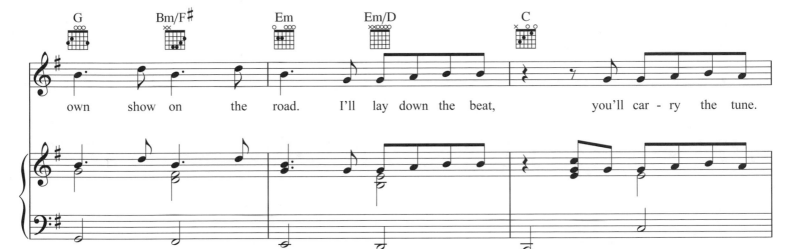

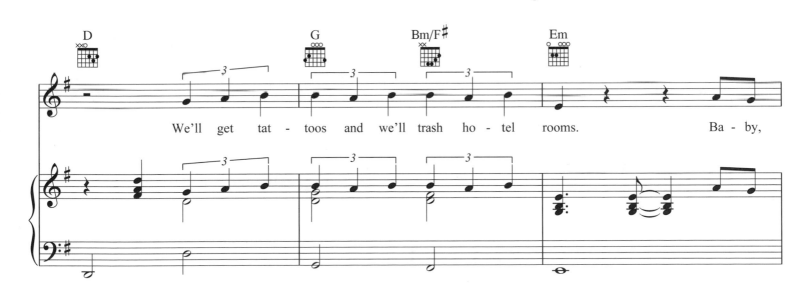

old jeans, and we'll nev - er learn how to sing the blues.

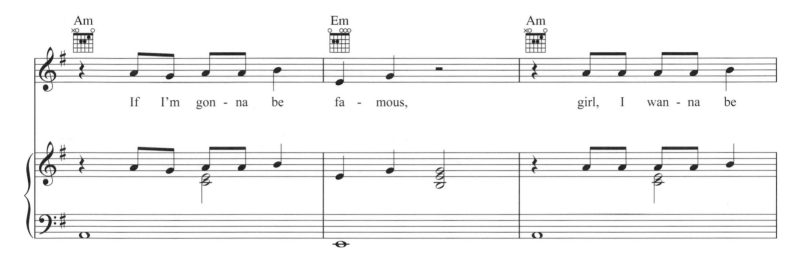

If I'm gon - na be fa - mous, girl, I wan - na be

fa - mous with you. We go our own lit - tle groove. I don't wan - na be a

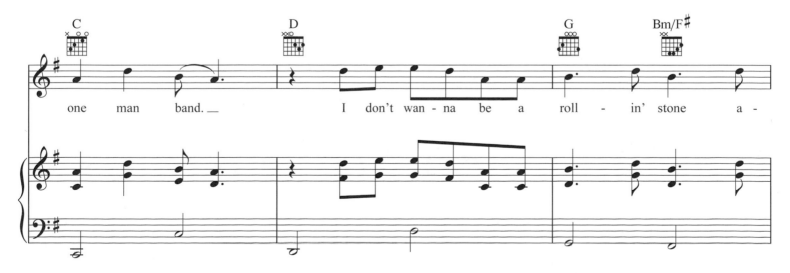

one man band. __ I don't wan - na be a roll - in' stone a -

lone, put - tin' miles __ on a run - down van. __ Ba - by, we can take our

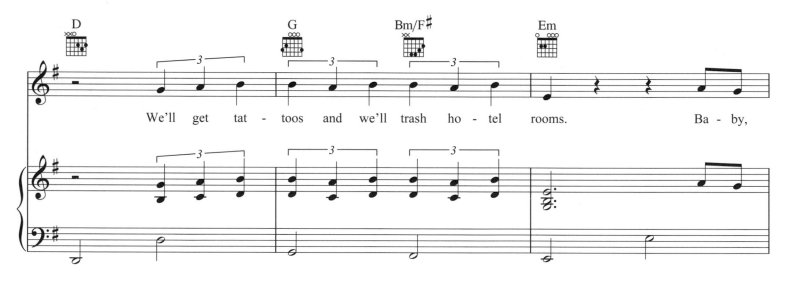

own show on the road. I'll lay down the beat, you'll car - ry the tune.

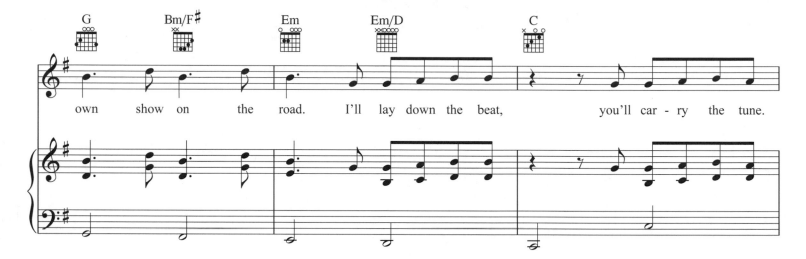

We'll get tat - toos and we'll trash ho - tel rooms. Ba - by,

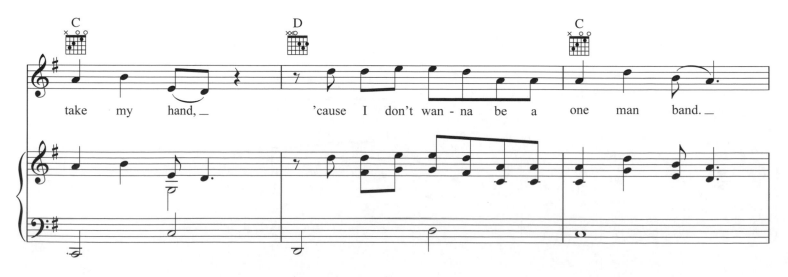

take my hand, __ 'cause I don't wan - na be a one man band. __

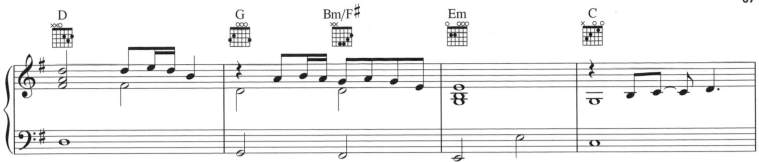

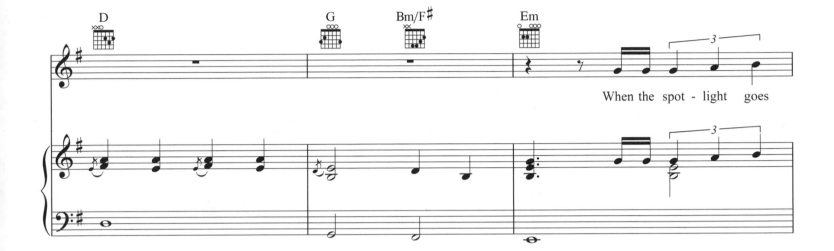

When the spot - light goes

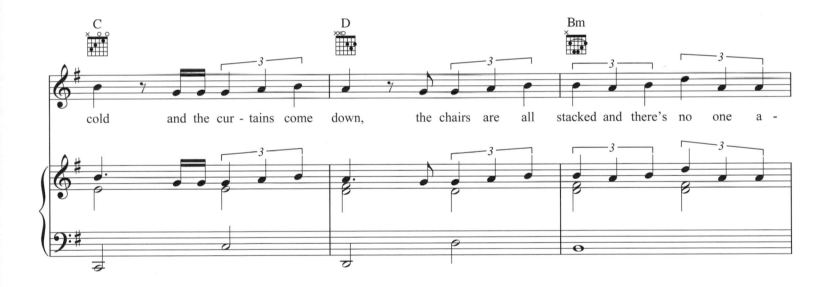

cold   and the cur - tains come down,   the chairs are all stacked and there's no one a -

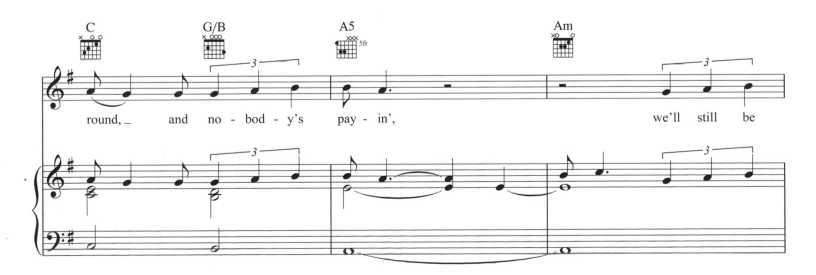

round, _   and no - bod - y's pay - in',   we'll still be

play - in'. I don't wan-na be a one man band. __

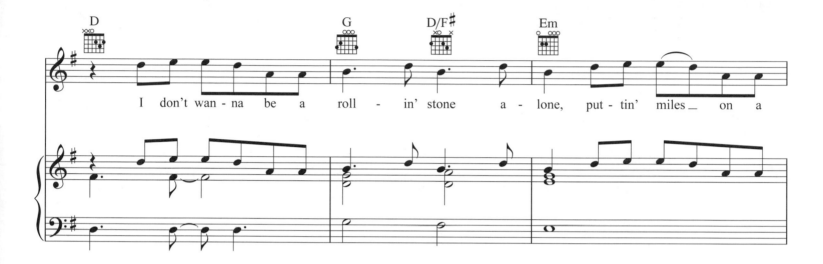

I don't wan-na be a roll - in' stone a - lone, put-tin' miles __ on a

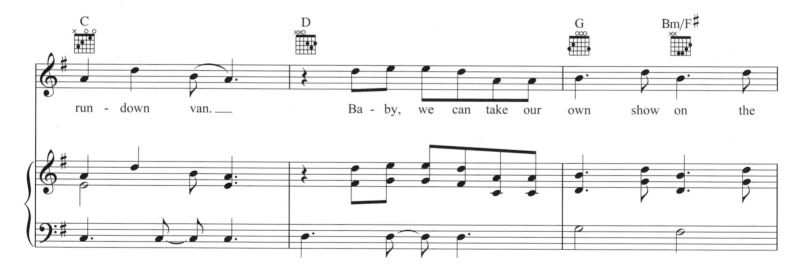

run - down van. __ Ba - by, we can take our own show on the

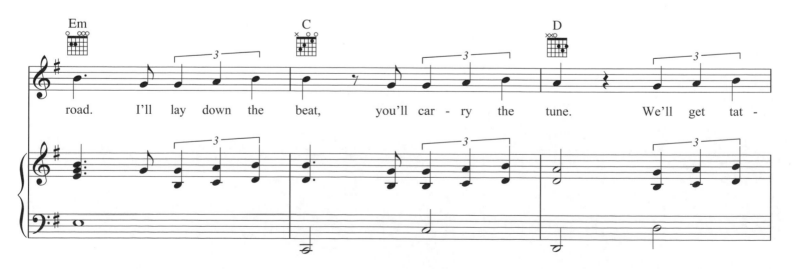

road. I'll lay down the beat, you'll car - ry the tune. We'll get tat -

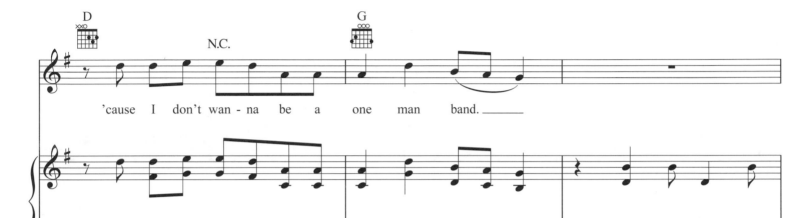

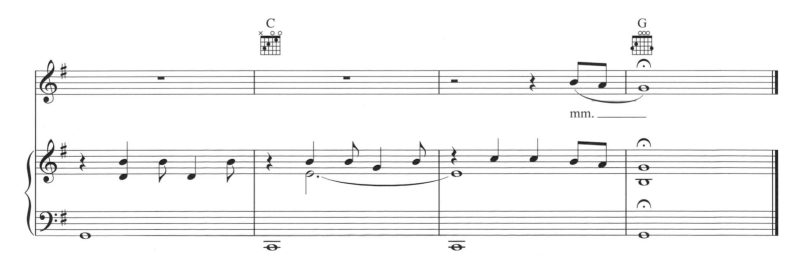

OLD TOWN ROAD
(Remix)

Words and Music by TRENT REZNOR,
BILLY RAY CYRUS, JOCELYN DONALD,
ATTICUS ROSS, KIOWA ROUKEMA
and MONTERO LAMAR HILL

Moderately

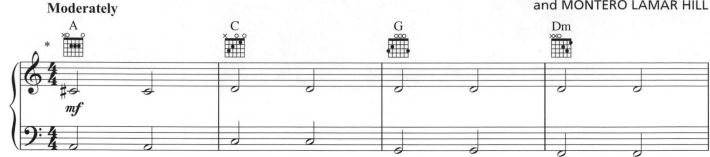

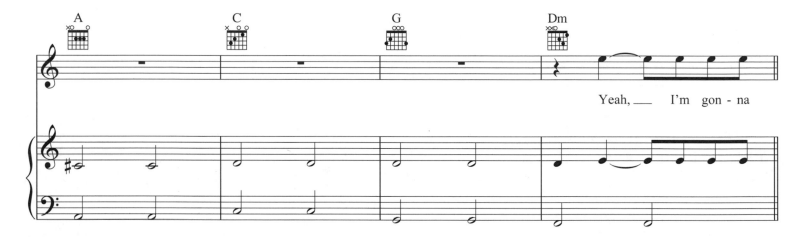

Yeah, ___ I'm gon-na

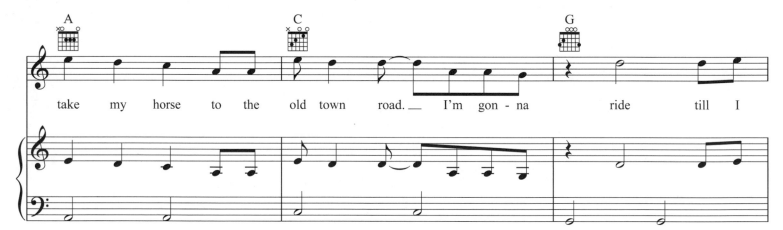

take my horse to the old town road. ___ I'm gon-na ride till I

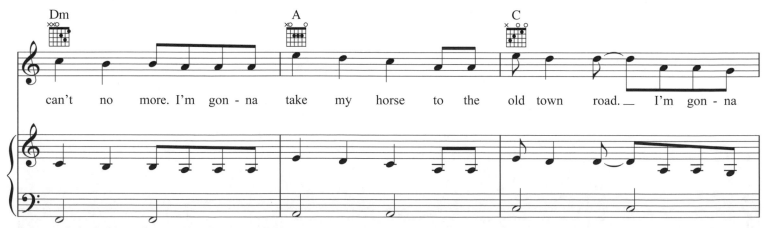

can't no more. I'm gon-na take my horse to the old town road. ___ I'm gon-na

* *Recorded a half step lower. Chords are implied.*

ride till I can't no more. I got the hors-es in the back, horse tack is at-tached.

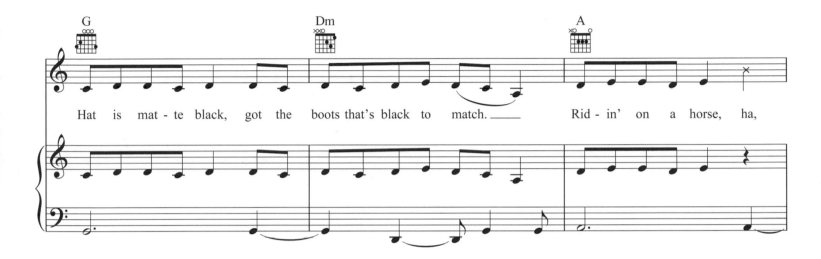

Hat is mat-te black, got the boots that's black to match. Rid-in' on a horse, ha,

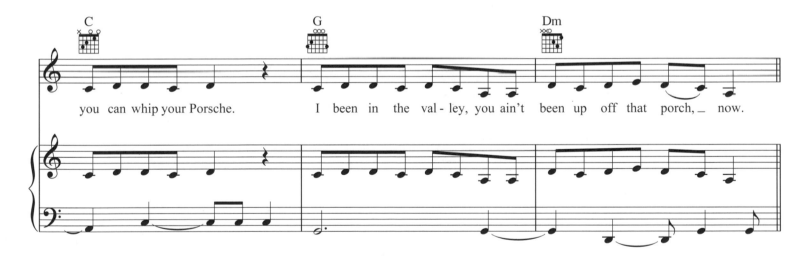

you can whip your Porsche. I been in the val-ley, you ain't been up off that porch, now.

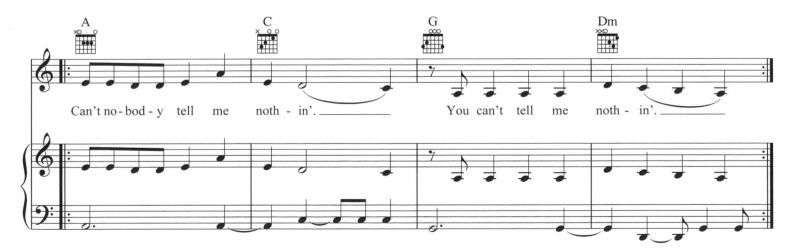

Can't no-bod-y tell me noth-in'. You can't tell me noth-in'.

Rid - in' on a trac - tor, lean all in my blad - der. Cheat - ed on my ba - by,

you can go and ask ___ her. My life is a mov - ie, bull rid - in' and boob - ies.

Cow - boy hat from Guc - ci, "Wran - gler" on my boot - y. Can't no - bod - y tell me

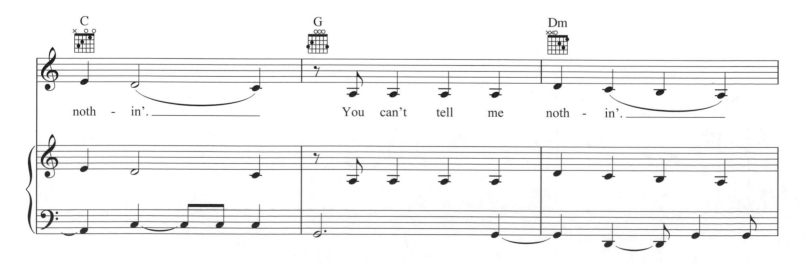

noth - in'. _____ You can't tell me noth - in'. _____

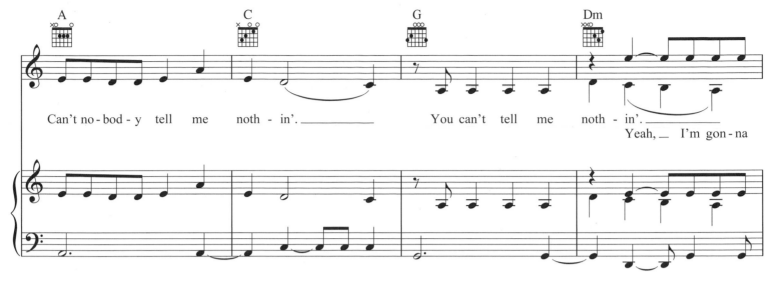

Can't no-bod-y tell me noth-in'. _____ You can't tell me noth-in'. _____
Yeah, _ I'm gon-na

take my horse to the old road town. _ I'm gon-na ride till I can't no more. I'm gon-na

take my horse to the old town road. _ I'm gon-na ride till I can't no more.

Hat down, cross town, liv-in' like a rock star. Spent a lot of mon-ey on my

brand - new gui - tar. Ba - by's got a hab - it: dia - mond rings and Fen - di sports bras.

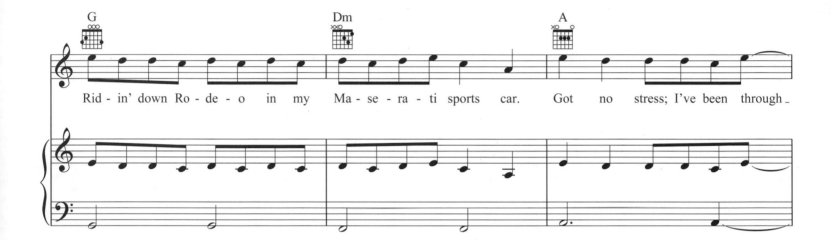

Rid - in' down Ro - de - o in my Ma - se - ra - ti sports car. Got no stress; I've been through___

___ all that.___ I'm like a Marl - boro Man, so I kick___ on back.___ Wish I could

roll on back to that old___ town road.___ I wan - na ride till I

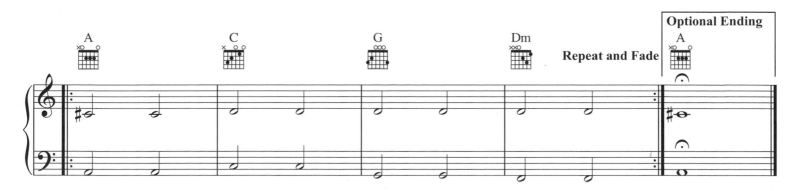

ONE THING RIGHT

Words and Music by MARSHMELLO,
MATTHEW McGINN, KANE BROWN,
JOSH HOGE and JESSE FRASURE

and _____ I've hurt, _____ I've bro - ken peo - ple down ___ with words. ___
right through ___ my pain, ___ kept us pa - tient while ___ I changed. ___

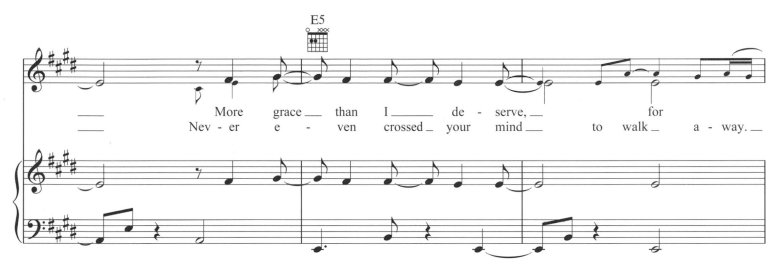

___ More grace ___ than I _____ de - serve, ___ for
Nev - er e - ven crossed ___ your mind ___ to walk ___ a - way. ___

sure. ___ Known to be cra - zy, known to be
___ When I was get - tin' cra - zy, reck - less and

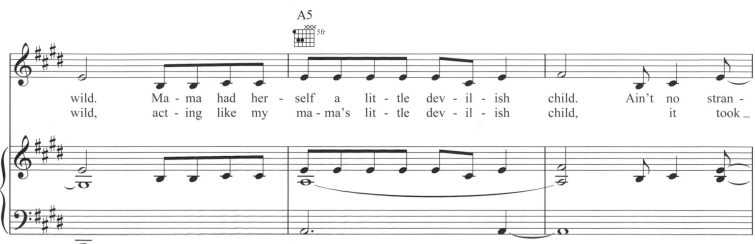

wild. Ma - ma had her - self a lit - tle dev - il - ish child. Ain't no stran -
wild, act - ing like my ma - ma's lit - tle dev - il - ish child, it took ___

D.S. al Coda

I got one ___ thing ___ right. ___ I've been at the

right. ___ I've been at the wrong place at the wrong time, chas-ing all the

wrong things most of my life. Been ev-'ry kind of lost that you ___ can't find, ___

___ but I ___ got one thing right. ___

PRAYED FOR YOU

Words and Music by MATTHEW STELL,
ASHLEY BOWERS and ALLISON VELTZ-CRUZ

Moderately slow, in 2

I've nev-er been one to ask ___ for help. ___

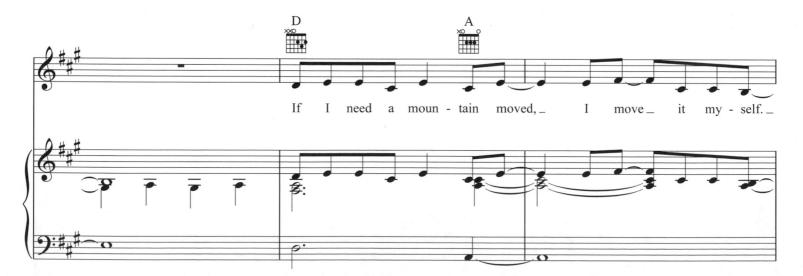

If I need a moun-tain moved, ___ I move ___ it my-self. ___

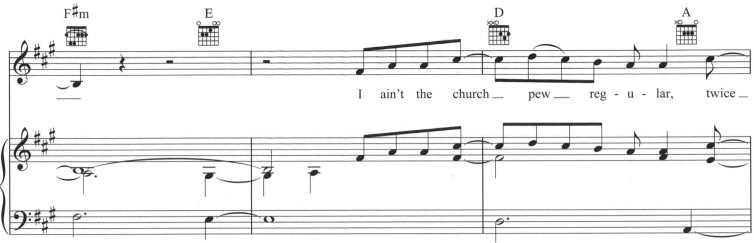

I ain't the church ___ pew ___ reg-u-lar, twice ___

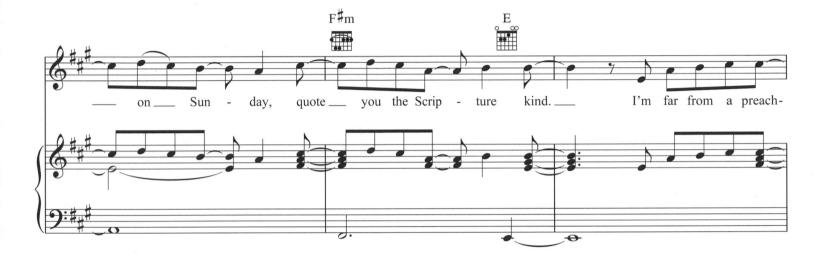

___ on ___ Sun-day, quote ___ you the Scrip-ture kind. ___ I'm far from a preach-

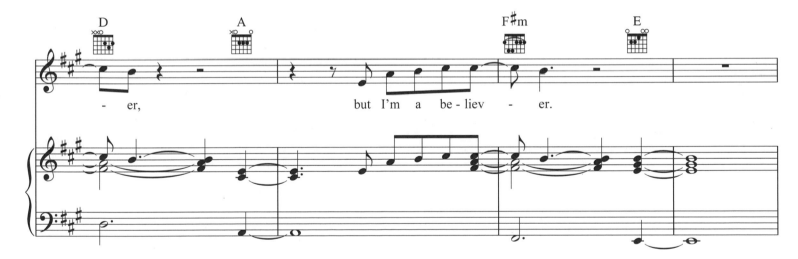

-er, but I'm a be-liev-er.

'Cause ev-'ry sin-gle day, ___ be-fore I knew your name, ___ I could-n't see your face, __

but I prayed for you. Ev-'ry heart-break trail, when all hope fell,

on the high-way to hell, I prayed for you. I kept my faith

like that old King James said I'm sup-posed to. It's

hard to i-mag-ine, big-ger than I could fath-om. I did-n't

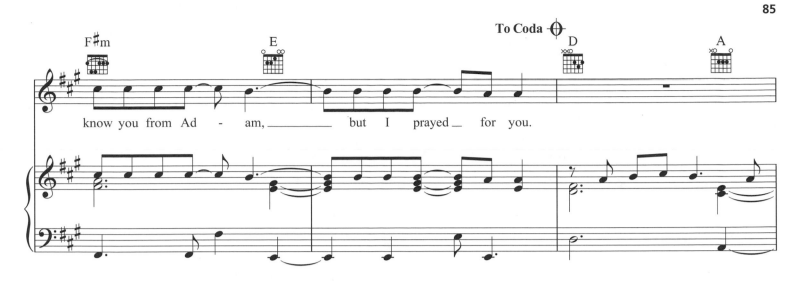

know you from Ad - am, _____ but I prayed _ for you.

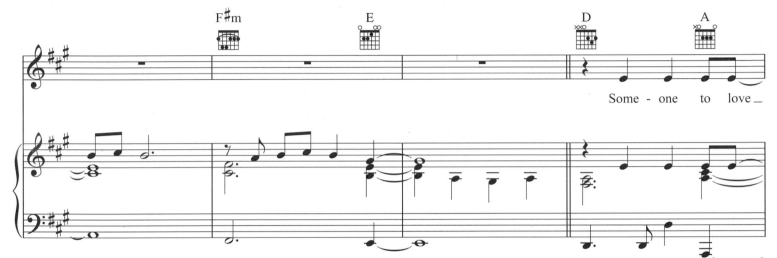

Some - one to love _

_____ me like _ you do.

Grace - ful eyes _____ to see _ me through. _

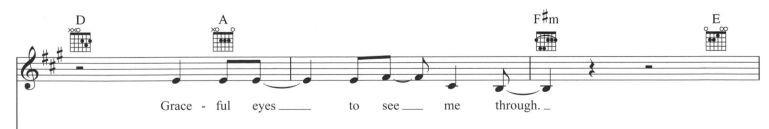

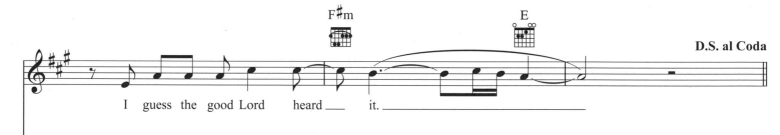

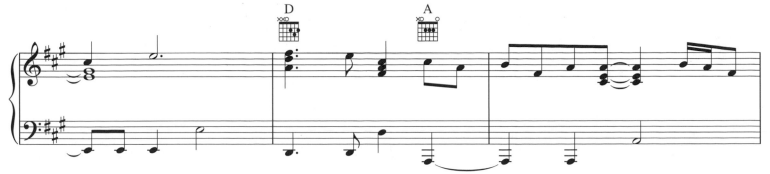

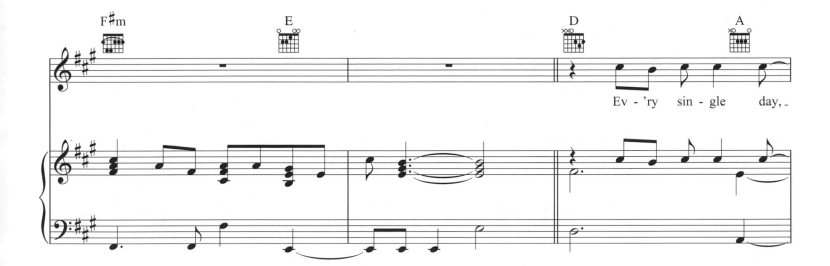

Ev - 'ry sin - gle day, _

_ be - fore I knew your name, _ I could-n't see your face, _ but I prayed _ for you.

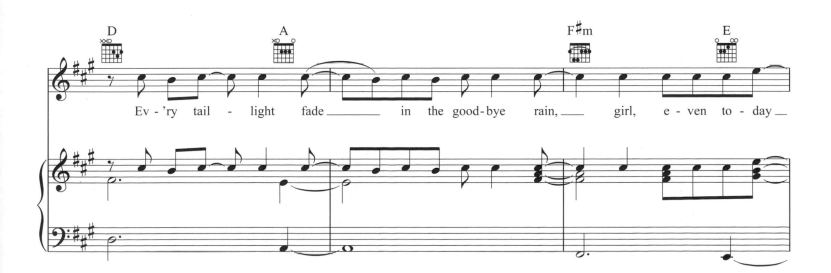

Ev - 'ry tail - light fade _ in the good-bye rain, _ girl, e - ven to - day _

I prayed _ for you. I kept _ my faith _ like that old _ King James _

said I'm _ sup - posed _ to. It's hard to i - mag _ - ine, big - ger

than I could fath - om. I did - n't know you from Ad - am, _

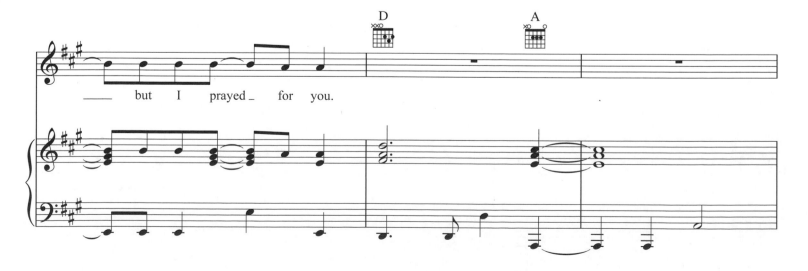

but I prayed _ for you.

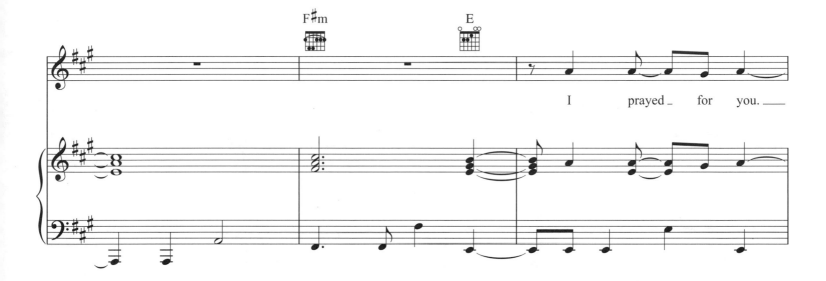

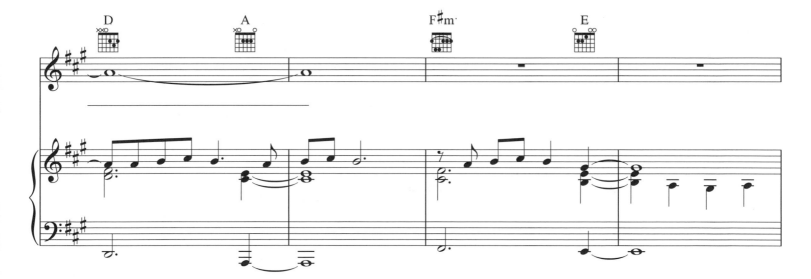

RAINBOW

Words and Music by KACEY MUSGRAVES,
SHANE McANALLY and NATALIE HEMBY

Piano Ballad

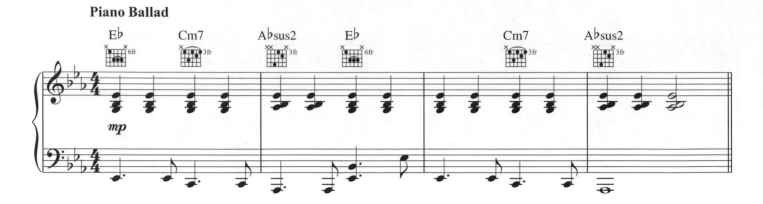

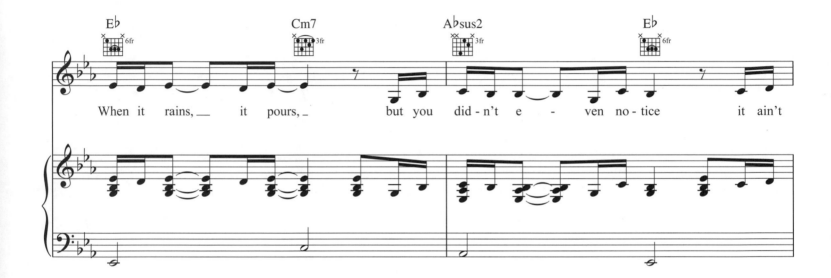

When it rains, ___ it pours, ___ but you did-n't e - ven no-tice it ain't

rain-ing an-y-more. ___ It's hard to breathe when all ___ you know is the

strug-gle of stay-ing ____ a-bove ___ the ris-ing wa-ter line. ____

____ Well, the sky has fi - n'lly o - pened, the

rain and wind _ stopped blow - ing. ___ But you're stuck out ____ in the same _ old storm a - gain. ___

____ You hold tight to your ___ um-brel - la. Well, dar - ling,

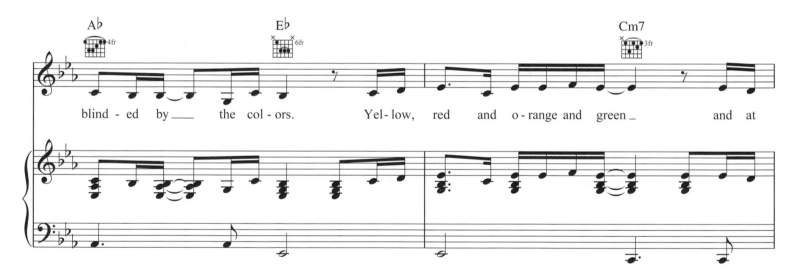

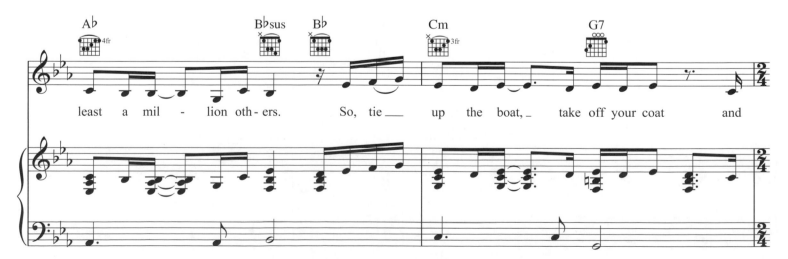

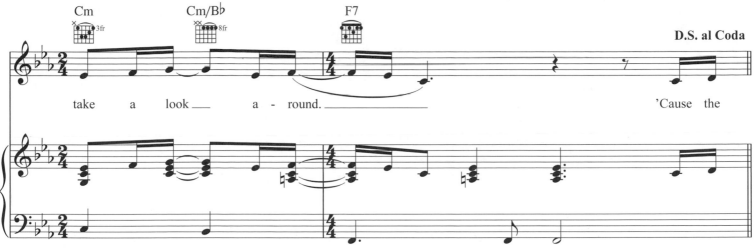

D.S. al Coda

take a look a - round. 'Cause the

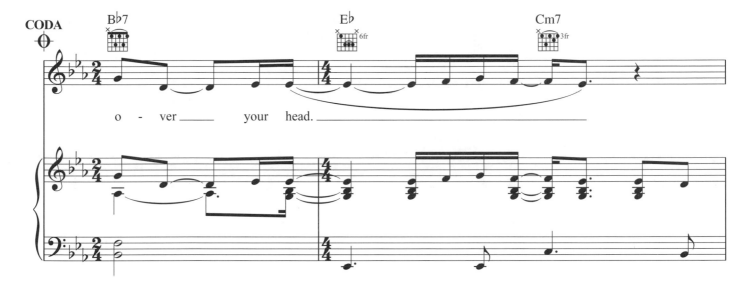

o - ver your head.

Oh, tie

up the boat, take off your coat and take a look a - round.

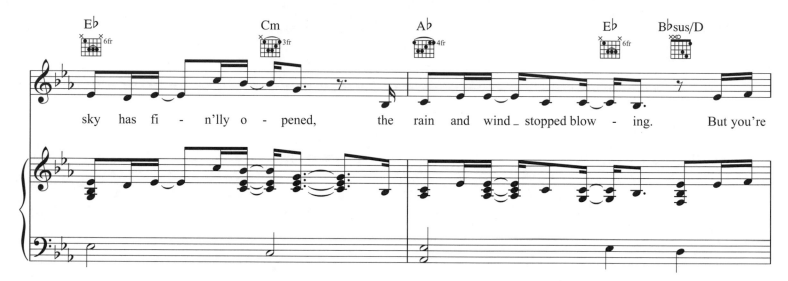

Ev - 'ry-thing is al - right now. __ 'Cause the

sky has fi - n'lly o - pened, the rain and wind __ stopped blow - ing. But you're

stuck out _____ in the same __ old storm a - gain. __ Let

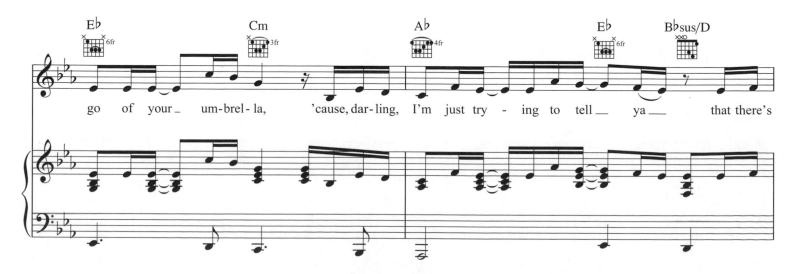

go of your __ um-brel - la, 'cause, dar - ling, I'm just try - ing to tell __ ya __ that there's

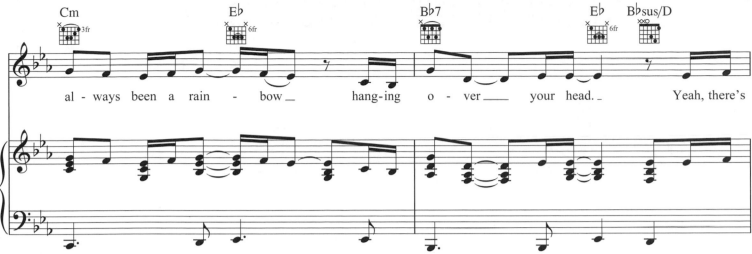

al - ways been a rain - bow ___ hang-ing o - ver ___ your head. ___ Yeah, there's

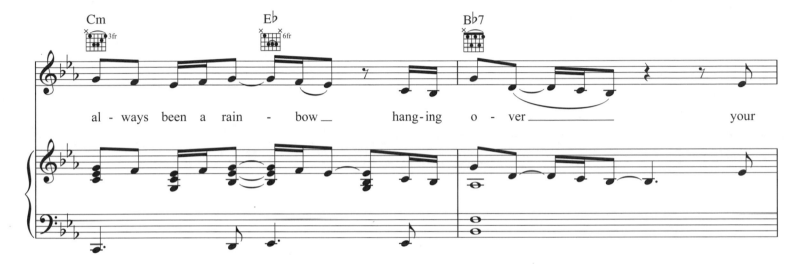

al - ways been a rain - bow ___ hang-ing o - ver _____ your

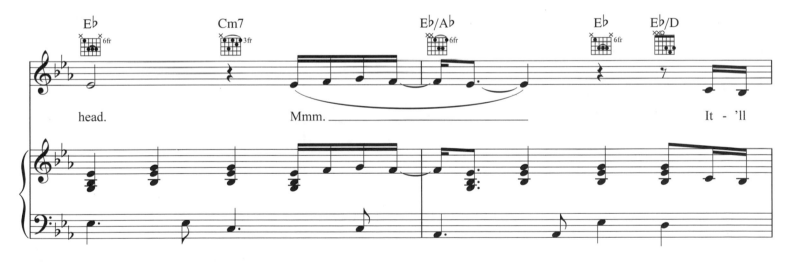

head. Mmm. _____ It - 'll

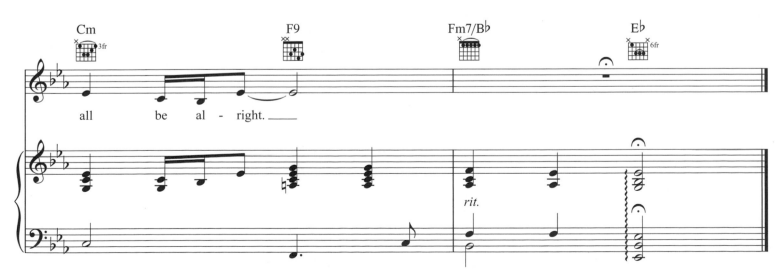

all be al - right. ___

REMEMBER YOU YOUNG

Words and Music by THOMAS RHETT,
ASHLEY GORLEY and JEESE FRASURE

Recorded a half step lower.

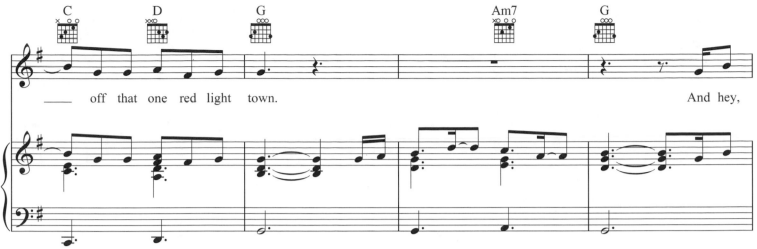

off that one red light town. And hey,

dar - lin', sip - pin' that red wine, all clas - sic, kicked back on the couch,

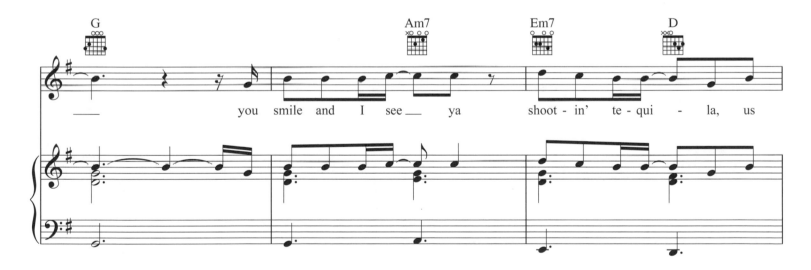

you smile and I see ya shoot - in' te - qui - la, us

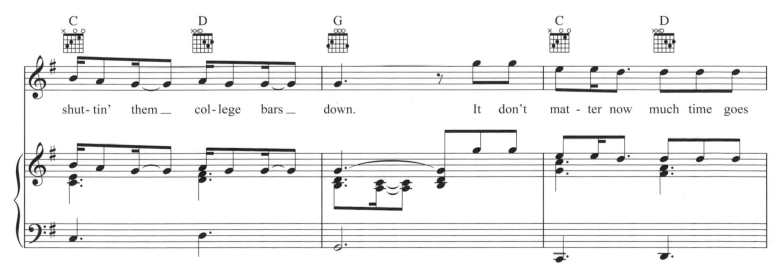

shut - tin' them col - lege bars down. It don't mat - ter now much time goes

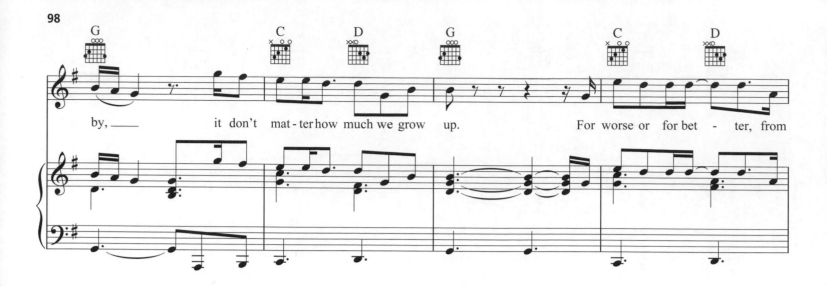

by, ____ it don't mat-ter how much we grow up. For worse or for bet - ter, from

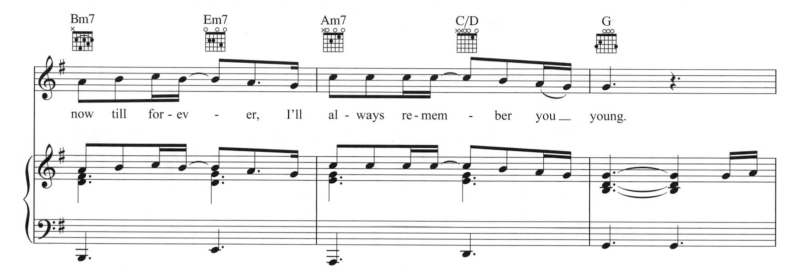

now till for - ev - er, I'll al - ways re - mem - ber you __ young.

Hey, ba - bies, crawl-in' on the car - pet, no, you

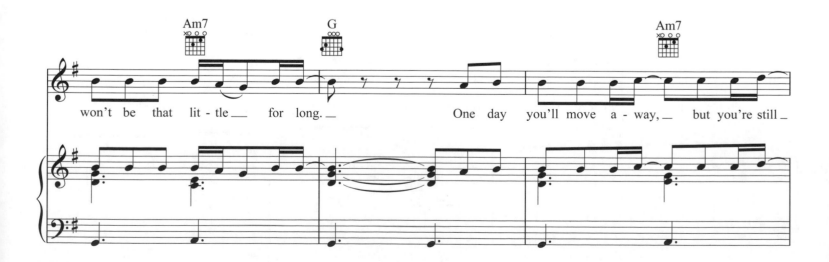

won't be that lit - tle __ for long. __ One day you'll move a - way, __ but you're still __

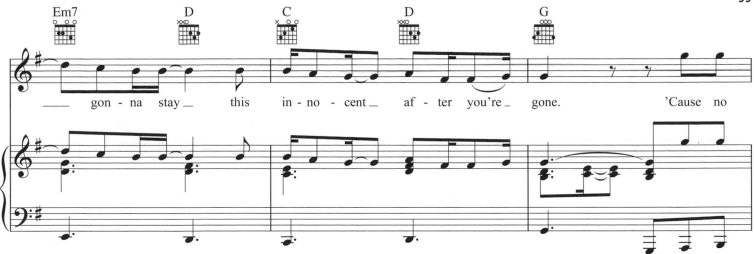

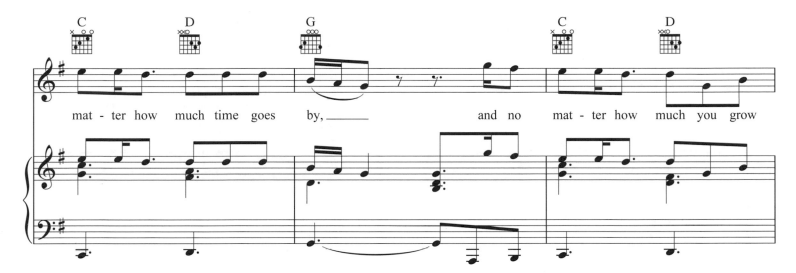

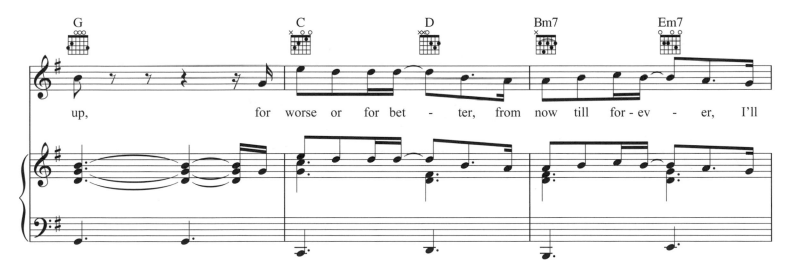

101

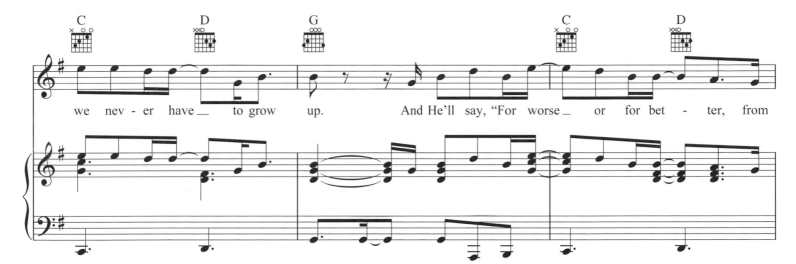

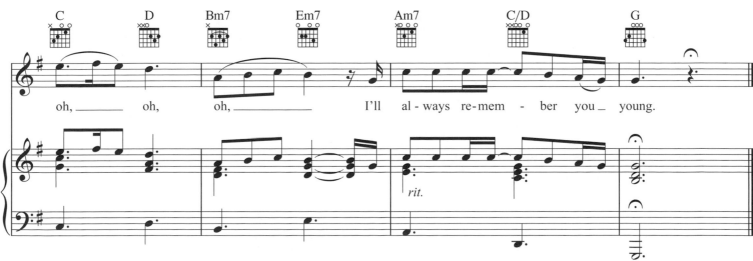

WHAT IF I NEVER GET OVER YOU

Words and Music by SAM ELLIS,
RYAN HURD, JONATHAN GREEN
and LAURA VELTZ

Moderate Country Pop feel

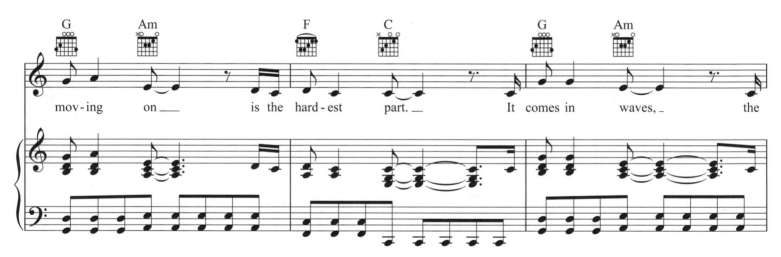

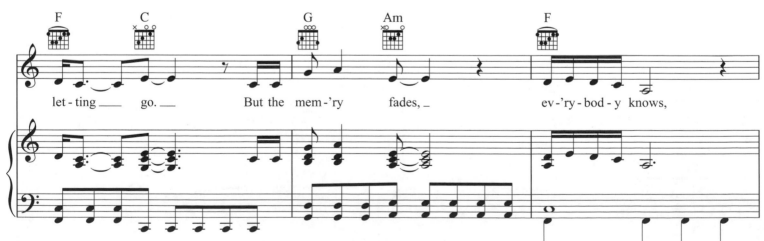

ev-'ry-bod-y knows. What if I'm try - ing, but then I close my __ eyes, __

__ and then I'm right back, lost in that last good - bye? __ What if time does-n't

do what it's sup-posed to do? __ What if I nev- er get o - ver you?

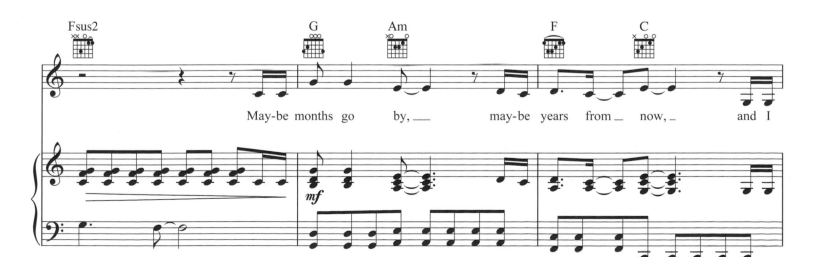

May-be months go by, __ may-be years from __ now, __ and I

meet some - one, _____ and it's work - ing out. _____ Ev - 'ry

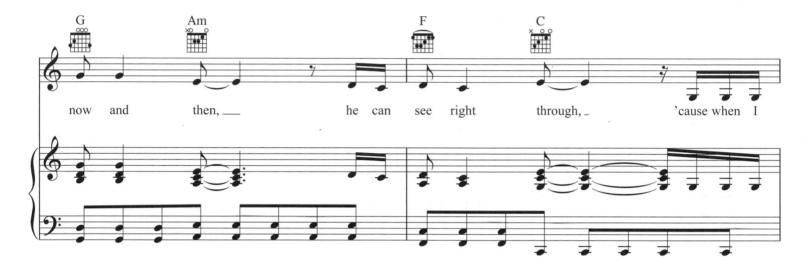

now and then, _____ he can see right through, _ 'cause when I

look at him, _ yeah, all I see is you. _

D.S. al Coda

CODA

nev - er get o - ver you?

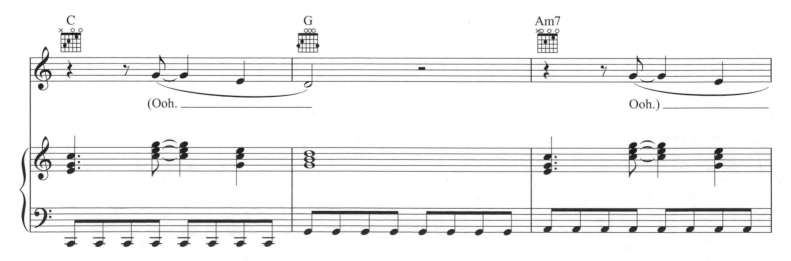

(Ooh. _____   Ooh.) _____

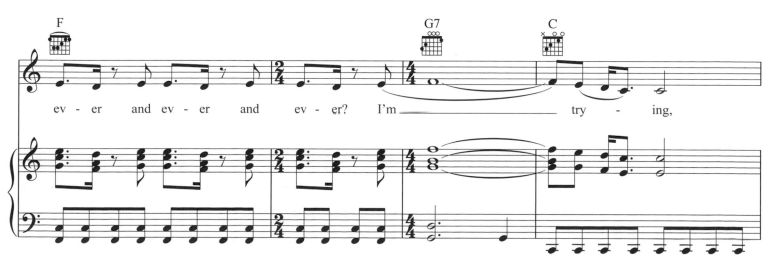

but then I close my eyes, and then I'm right back, lost in that last good - bye.

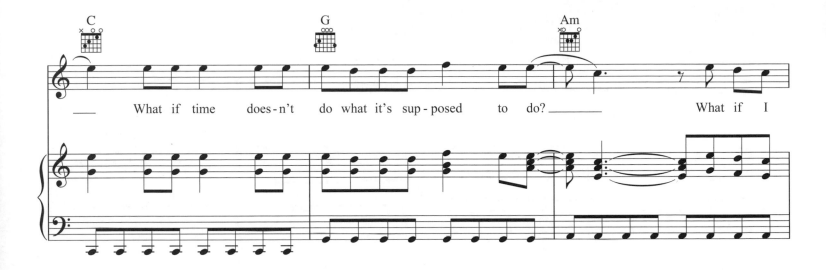

What if time does-n't do what it's sup-posed to do? What if I

nev - er get o - ver you? What if I gave you ev - 'ry - thing I've got?

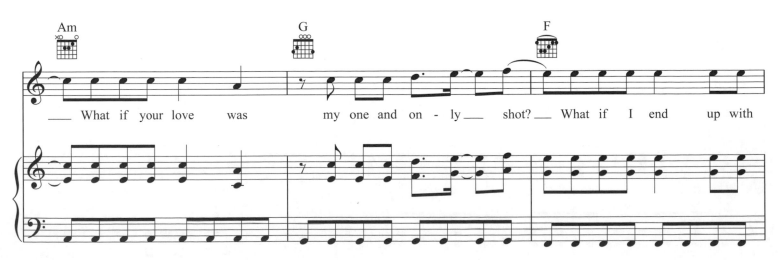

What if your love was my one and on - ly shot? What if I end up with

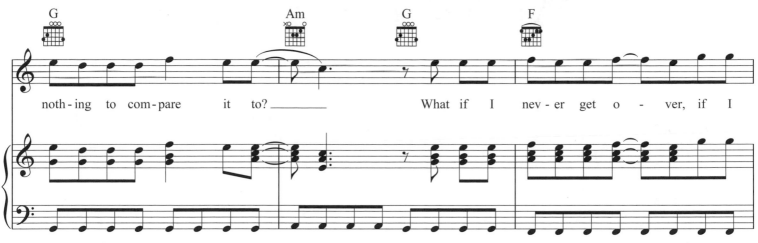

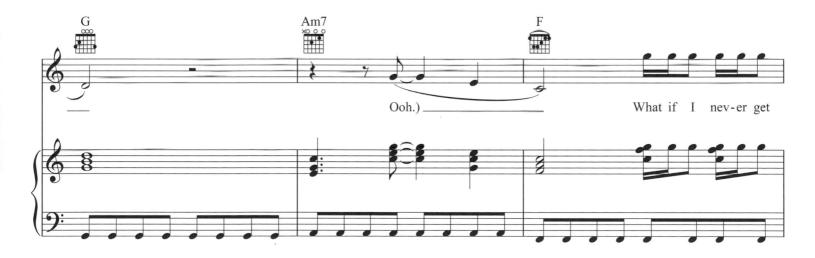

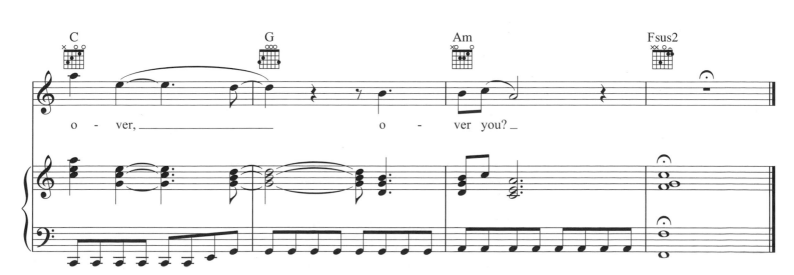

WHISKEY GLASSES

Words and Music by KEVIN KADISH
and BEN BURGESS

* *Recorded a half step lower.*

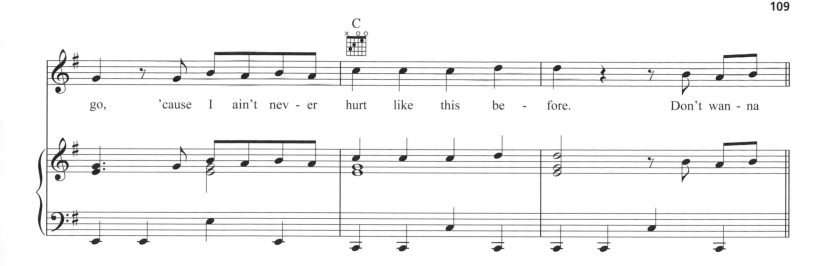

go, 'cause I ain't nev - er hurt like this be - fore. Don't wan - na

think a - bout __ her or wear a ring with - out __ her. Don't wan - na

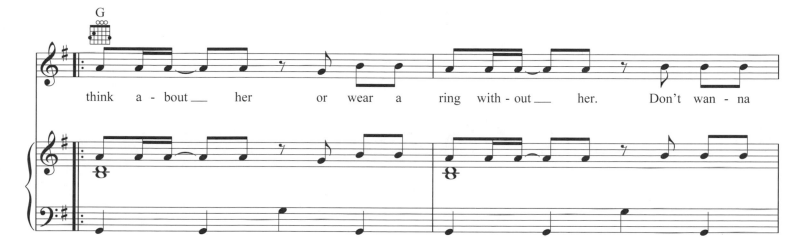

hit the kar - a - o - ke bar; __ can't sing with - out her. So, make them drinks strong, __ 'cause, broth - er,

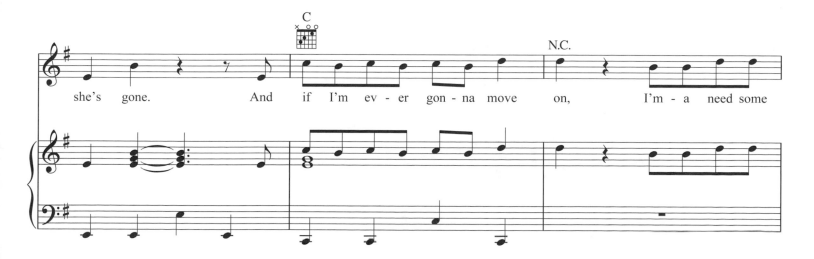

she's gone. And if I'm ev - er gon - na move on, I'm - a need some

whis - key glass - es, 'cause I don't wan - na see the truth._____

She's prob-'ly mak- in' out on the couch right now with_ some - one new.

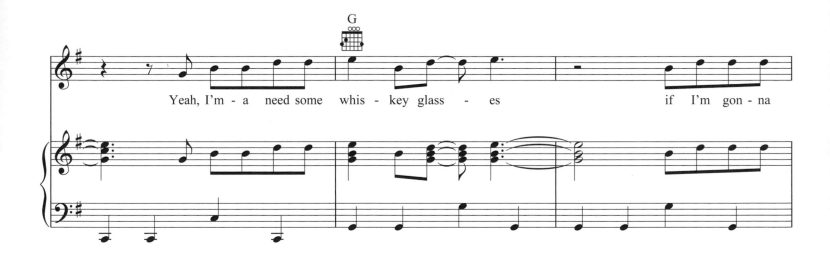

Yeah, I'm - a need some whis - key glass - es if I'm gon - na

make it through._____ If I'm - a be sin - gle, I'm - a

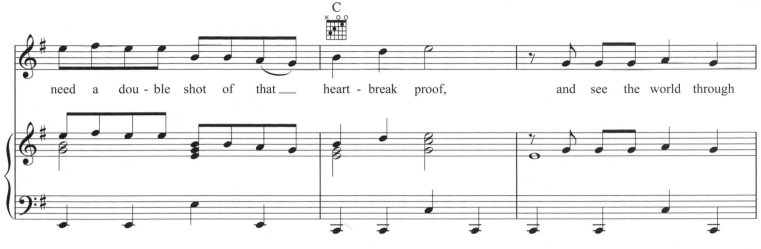

need a dou-ble shot of that ___ heart-break proof, and see the world through

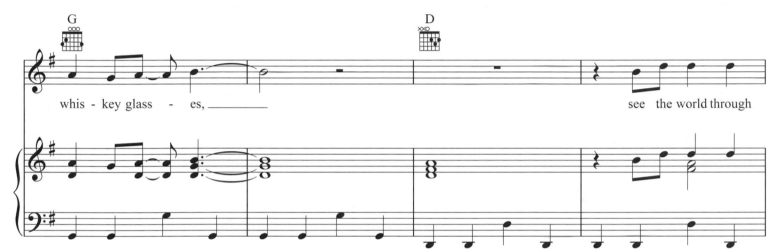

whis-key glass - es, ___ see the world through

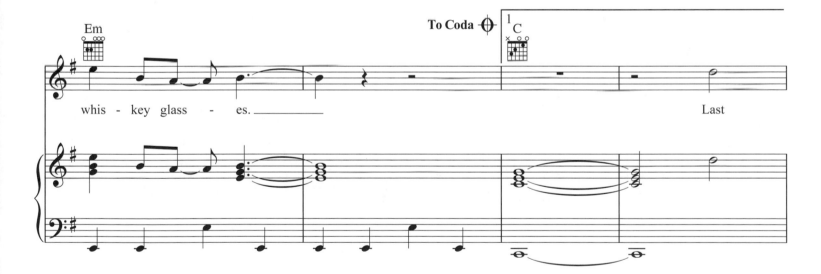

whis-key glass - es. ___ Last

To Coda

call, ___ I swear ___ this-'ll be my last call. Now,

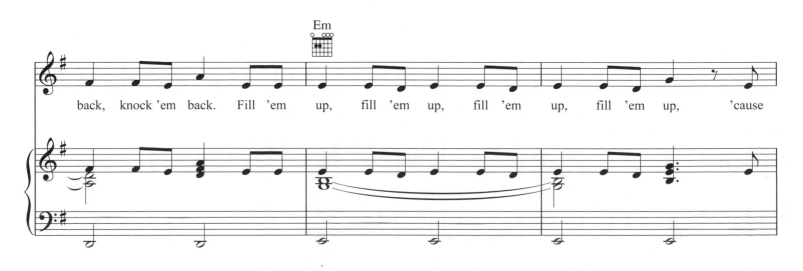

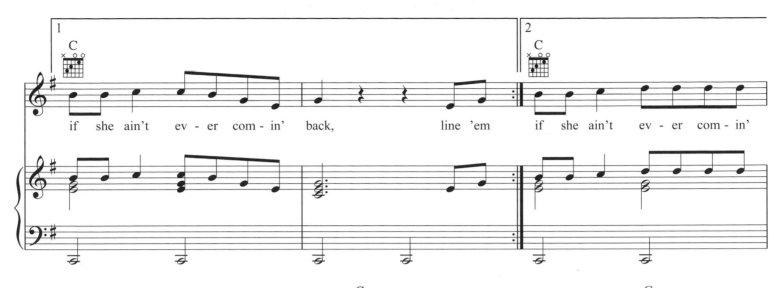

if she ain't ev - er com - in' back, line 'em if she ain't ev - er com - in'

D.S. al Coda

back, __ I'm - a need some

CODA

Yeah. _____

See the world through whis - key glass - es, _____

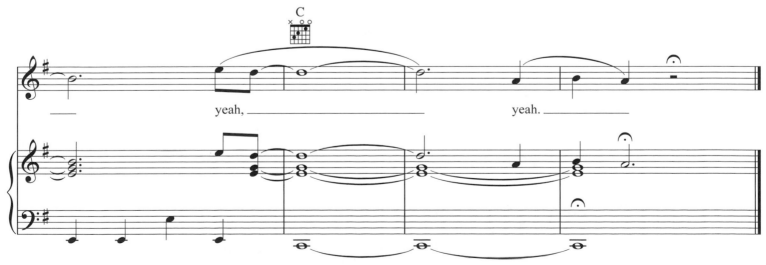

yeah, _____ yeah. _____

10,000 HOURS

Words and Music by DAN SMYERS,
JORDAN REYNOLDS, SHAY MOONEY,
JUSTIN BIEBER, JASON BOYD
and JESSIE JO DILLON

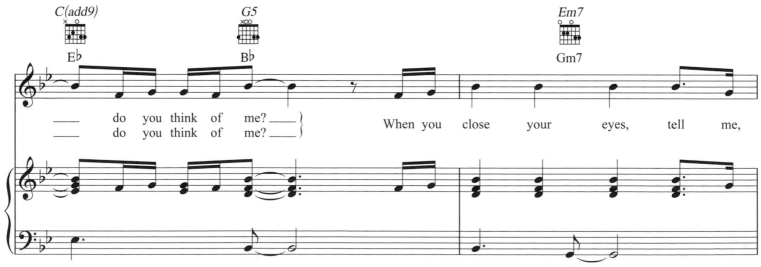

what are you dream-ing? Ev-'ry-thing, I wan-na know it all,_____ mmm.__ I'd spend

ten thou-sand ho - urs__ and ten thou-sand more,__ oh, if that's what it takes_ to learn that

sweet heart of yours.__ And I might nev-er get__ there,__ but I'm gon-na try,_____ if it's

Ooh, _____ want the good and the bad, ev-'ry-thing in be-tween. _____

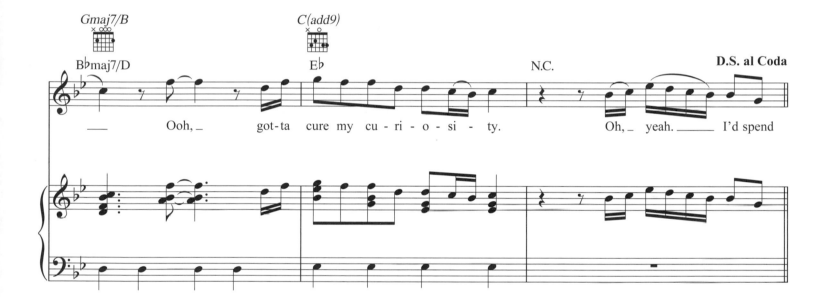

Ooh, _ got-ta cure my cu-ri-o-si-ty. Oh,_ yeah. _____ I'd spend

D.S. al Coda

rest of my life. _____ I'm gon-na love _____ you. Ooh. _____

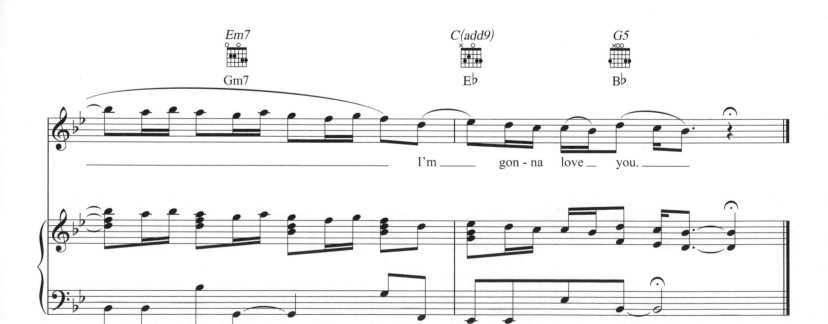

Contemporary & Classic Country

More great country hits from Hal Leonard arranged for piano and voice with guitar chords.

#1 Country Hits of the 2000s
28 megahits by 19 of the finest artists of the decade! Songs include: Bless the Broken Road • Breathe • I Hope You Dance • Live like You Were Dying • Love Story • Our Song • Redneck Woman • Want To • When the Sun Goes Down • Where Were You (When the World Stopped Turning) • and more.
00311951 .... $16.99

The Best Country Songs Ever – 3rd Edition
This outstanding collection features 76 country favorites: Always on My Mind • Blue • Could I Have This Dance • Daddy Sang Bass • Friends in Low Places • God Bless the U.S.A. • I Fall to Pieces • Love Without End, Amen • Mammas Don't Let Your Babies Grow Up to Be Cowboys • Rhinestone Cowboy • Stand by Your Man • Wabash Cannonball • more.
00359135 .... $27.99

Country Songs – Budget Book
You get a lot of bang for your buck with this great collection of 90 songs for only $14.99! Titles include: All My Ex's Live in Texas • Boot Scootin' Boogie • Cowboy Take Me Away • Elvira • Hey, Good Lookin' • Lucille • Okie from Muskogee • Sixteen Tons • and many more!
00310833 .... $14.99

Country Songs of Faith, Hope & Love – 2nd Edition
22 favorites for piano, voice and guitar: Angels Among Us • Believe • Bless the Broken Road • God Gave Me You • Hello World • I Hope You Dance • If Heaven Wasn't So Far Away • Jesus Take the Wheel • Long Black Train • The Man I Want to Be • Savior's Shadow • Something in the Water • Three Wooden Crosses • When I Get Where I'm Goin' • and more.
00159863 .... $14.99

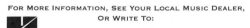
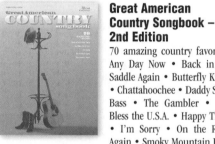

The Great American Songbook – Country
MUSIC AND LYRICS FOR 100 CLASSIC SONGS
Abilene • Always on My Mind • Are You Lonesome Tonight? • Blue Bayou • Breathe • Butterfly Kisses • Can the Circle Be Unbroken • Cold, Cold Heart • Desperado • The Devil Went Down to Georgia • The Gambler • God Bless the U.S.A. • I Swear • Jolene • The Keeper of the Stars • On the Road Again • Rocky Top • You Don't Know Me • Your Cheatin' Heart • and scores more!
00110386 .... $34.99

Great American Country Songbook – 2nd Edition
70 amazing country favorites: Any Day Now • Back in the Saddle Again • Butterfly Kisses • Chattahoochee • Daddy Sang Bass • The Gambler • God Bless the U.S.A. • Happy Trails • I'm Sorry • On the Road Again • Smoky Mountain Rain • Your Cheatin' Heart • dozens more!
00359947 .... $19.95

Inspirational Country Hits
Nearly 30 country-flavored inspirational favorites, including: Better Than I Used to Be • Don't Blink • God Gave Me You • Hello World • I Won't Let Go • If Heaven Wasn't So Far Away • Live like You Were Dying • Temporary Home • Time Is Love • and more.
00112961 .... $16.99

The Most Requested Country Love Songs
Fifty-nine romantic renderings by country crooners: Always on My Mind • Amazed • Butterfly Kisses • Crazy • Forever and Ever, Amen • He Stopped Loving Her Today • I Swear • I Will Always Love You • Love Story • Making Memories of Us • One More Day • Stand by Your Man • Through the Years • When You Say Nothing at All • You're Still the One • and more.
00159649 .... $22.99

100 Greatest Country Artists
100 SONGS BY 100 ARTISTS
This jam-packed collection salutes 100 of the brightest stars of country music, honoring each of them with one song arranged for piano, voice and guitar. Includes: Alabama (Mountain Music) • Johnny Cash (Ring of Fire) • Kenny Chesney (Come Over) • Brad Paisley (She's Everything) • Chris Stapleton (Tennessee Whiskey) • Shania Twain (Man! I Feel like a Woman!) • Carrie Underwood (Before He Cheats) • Keith Urban (Blue Ain't Your Color) • and many more.
00250372 .... $27.99

COUNTRY MUSIC TELEVISION'S 100 Greatest Songs of Country Music
In 2003, Country Music Television compiled a panel of experts to rank the 100 greatest country songs of all time. This folio presents all 100 songs: Crazy (#3) • Friends in Low Places (#6) • He Stopped Loving Her Today (#2) • Ring of Fire (#4) • Stand by Your Man (#1) • Your Cheatin' Heart (#5) • and many more.
00306544 .... $32.99

Roadhouse Country
30 FAVORITE SONGS
30 songs sure to be crowd favorites in country bars across the country. Includes: All My Ex's Live in Texas • Coal Miner's Daughter • El Paso • Folsom Prison Blues • Hey, Good Lookin' • Jolene • King of the Road • Mama Tried • On the Road Again • Take This Job and Shove It • White Lightning • and more.
00248528 .... $14.99

Today's Women of Country – 2nd Edition
This second edition has been updated to include hits by today's top female artists. Songs include: Before He Cheats • The House That Built Me • A Little Bit Stronger • Love Story • Mean • Need You Now • Stuck like Glue • You Lie • and more.
00310446 .... $14.99

Country Sheet Music 2010-2019
40 of the hottest country hits from the decade in arrangements for piano, voice and guitar. Songs include: American Honey • Cruise • Drinkin' Problem • Homesick • If I Die Young • Marry Me • Ridin' Roads • Stuck like Glue • Wanted • Yours • and more.
00345260 .... $22.99

Wedding Songs Country Style – 2nd Edition
An excellent selection of 35 popular "country style" wedding and love songs. New, old and unique songs are featured. Includes: The Keeper of the Stars • Marry Me • Grow Old with Me • One Boy, One Girl • Vows Go Unbroken • When You Say Nothing at All • and many others.
00310183 .... $14.95

TOP COUNTRY HITS

Arranged for piano and voice with guitar chords.

Top Country Hits of 2019-2020

18 of the best country songs from 2019 to 2020: All to Myself • Beer Never Broke My Heart • The Bones • Even Though I'm Leaving • Girl • God's Country • I Don't Know About You • Look What God Gave Her • Miss Me More • Old Town Road (Remix) • One Man Band • One Thing Right • Prayed for You • Rainbow • Remember You Young • 10,000 Hours • What If I Never Get over You • Whiskey Glasses.

00334223 ....$17.99

Top Country Hits of 2018-2019

18 Hot Singles

18 of the year's hottest country hits arranged for piano, voice and guitar. Includes: Best Shot (Jimmie Allen) • Drowns the Whiskey (Jason Aldean) • Get Along (Kenny Chesney) • Hangin' On (Chris Young) • Heaven (Kane Brown) • Love Wins (Carrie Underwood) • Mercy (Brett Young) • Rich (Maren Morris) • She Got the Best of Me (Luke Combs) • Simple (Florida Georgia Line) • Up Down (Morgan Wallen feat. Florida Georgia Line) • and more.

00289814 ....$17.99

Top Country Hits of 2017-2018

18 of the year's top toe-tapping, twangy hits: Body like a Back Road • Broken Halos • Craving You • Dear Hate • Dirt on My Boots • Dirty Laundry • Drinkin' Problem • Fighter • Hurricane • Legends • Meant to Be • Millionaire • Yours • and more.

00267160 ....$17.99

Top Country Hits of 2015-2016

14 of the year's most popular country songs: Burning House (Cam) • Biscuits (Kacey Musgraves) • Girl Crush (Little Big Town) • I'm Comin' Over (Chris Young) • Let Me See You Girl (Cole Swindell) • Smoke Break (Carrie Underwood) • Strip It Down (Luke Bryan) • Take Your Time (Sam Hunt) • Traveller (Chris Stapleton) • and more.

00156297 ....$16.99

Top Country Hits of 2014-2015

14 of the year's most popular country songs. Includes: American Kids (Kenny Chesney) • Day Drinking (Little Big Town) • I See You (Luke Bryan) • Neon Light (Blake Shelton) • Payback (Rascal Flatts) • Shotgun Rider (Tim McGraw) • Something in the Water (Carrie Underwood) • Sunshine & Whiskey (Frankie Ballard) • Talladega (Eric Church) • and more.

00142574 ....$16.99

Top Country Hits of 2013-2014

15 of today's most recognizable hits from country's hottest stars, including: Carolina (Parmalee) • Cruise (Florida Georgia Line) • Drunk Last Night (Eli Young Band) • Mine Would Be You (Blake Shelton) • Southern Girl (Tim McGraw) • That's My Kind of Night (Luke Bryan) • We Were Us (Keith Urban and Miranda Lambert) • and more.

00125359 ....$16.99

Top Country Hits of 2012-2013

Features 15 fantastic country hits: Beer Money • Begin Again • Better Dig Two • Come Wake Me Up • Every Storm (Runs Out of Rain) • Fastest Girl in Town • Hard to Love • Kiss Tomorrow Goodbye • The One That Got Away • Over You • Red • Take a Little Ride • Til My Last Day • Wanted • We Are Never Ever Getting Back Together.

00118291 ....$14.99

HAL•LEONARD®

Prices, content and availability subject to change without notice.

0120
232